FILE ON THE SHROUD

The Reverend H. David Sox has had an interest in the Turin Shroud since 1956 when he visited Turin on his way to work at an ecumenical work camp in the area sponsored by the World Council of Churches. In 1977 he arranged the first conference to be held in Britain on the subject of the Turin Shroud. He is a personal friend of King Umberto II, the owner of the relic, and has become involved with the current attempts to get the Shroud carbon-dated and further tested. He has written articles on the subject for the American Episcopal press, *The Tablet, The Catholic Herald, New Realities* and *The Clergy Review*.

Along with his clergy and teaching duties, Sox is the General Secretary of the British Society for the Turin Shroud.

File on the Shroud

H. David Sox

CORONET BOOKS
Hodder and Stoughton

Copyright © 1978 by H. David Sox

First published in Great Britain 1978 by Coronet Books

This book is sold subject to the condition that it shall not, by way of trade or otherwise, be lent, re-sold, hired out or otherwise circulated without the publisher's prior consent in any form of binding or cover other than that in which this is published and without a similar condition including this condition being imposed on the subsequent purchaser.

Printed and bound in Great Britain for Hodder and Stoughton Paperbacks, a division of Hodder and Stoughton Ltd., Mill Road, Dunton Green, Sevenoaks, Kent (Editorial Office: 47 Bedford Square, London, WC1 3DP) by C. Nicholls & Company Ltd
The Philips Park Press, Manchester

ISBN 0 340 24211 6

For my parents and Allan who have had to endure much of my efforts regarding the Turin Shroud

CONTENTS

Foreword by Sir Steven Runciman

Preface

1	What Is the Shroud of Turin?	15
2	What Do the Gospels Say about the Shroud?	21
3	What Is the Shroud's History?	39
4	What Has Science Said about the Shroud in the Past?	60
5	Did Jesus Die on the Cross?	75
6	What Did Scientists Say about the Shroud 1969 – 1977?	84
7	How Was the Shroud Brought to the Tests in 1978?	117
8	Can This Be Jesus?	143

FOREWORD

Amongst all the relics that Christians have revered down the centuries, the Holy Shroud of Turin is unique. Not many of the objects that sanctified the shrines of medieval Europe are still in existence. Some have been destroyed by fire or lost in war. Some were deliberately destroyed at the Reformation, or during the French Revolution, when the great collection in the Sainte Chapelle in Paris was hacked to pieces. Some have just disappeared, unnoted and not much regretted. Few of them had origins that could be verified or histories that could be traced. We can follow the career of the great relics of the Passion which the Empress Helena unearthed at Calvary and which remained for many centuries in Constantinople and then were transferred to the Sainte Chapelle, though we cannot prove that the crosses that the Imperial archaeologist discovered were truly those on which Christ and the thieves suffered. There are relics of the saints which were removed from their actual tombs and whose authenticity is thus fairly well assured. But most of the others depend for their acceptance on simple uncritical faith. There is no harm in that. An object that countless generations have regarded as holy surely acquires some holiness and is worthy of respect. Nothing is gained by pouring scorn on obviously dubious origins.

The Holy Shroud fits into none of these categories. It is claimed not only to be the very shroud in which Our Lord's body was wrapped but to bear on it the imprint of His face and body; and those to whom permission is given can see for themselves that indeed it bears the imprint of a human face and form. If the claim is genuine, the importance of the Shroud for the historic truth of the Gospels is clearly enormous. But is the claim to be accepted? The history of the Shroud can be accurately traced from the mid-fourteenth century; but where was so venerable a relic before that date? Attempts to identify it with a known relic of an earlier date, such as the Image of Edessa have not, I think, been successful. It is tempting to identify it with the shroud with an imprint on it that the Crusader Robert de Clari saw just before the Latin sack of Constantinople in 1204. But he says that the relic was lost then. Moreover such a shroud was never mentioned by the Byzantines, though they claimed to have the shroud of Christ, nor is it mentioned by any of the pilgrims who came to see the famed relic-collections of Constantinople. It is true that to the Byzantines the really important relics were those of the Passion, the cruel instruments of our salvation. The shroud would be of less significance. But a shroud that depicted the face and body of Our Lord would hardly have been ignored. The historical background is not satisfactory. There is a question of iconography over the beard. There is the question of how exactly burial clothes were fixed at that time. There are problems that the scientists may be able to solve for us, of dating and of the nature of the pigments. But even if the dating of the linen is fixed, there are still questions. We are told that seeds have shown that the linen comes from the East; but medieval Europe imported linen from the East. The linen may be proved to be old; but a clever forger might have secured a piece of old linen on which to work, just as modern forgers of icons choose pieces of old wood. The fourteenth century was an age when the forgery of relics was rampant. Many people even then thought the Shroud to be a forgery. Modern techniques may add to our information; but can we ever know the entire truth?

Perhaps the Holy Shroud should be left as a mystery, safe in its holiness because of the accumulated reverence that has been paid to it by the faithful. But modern churchmen are afraid of mystery. They desire that all theology should be brought into the finite sphere of human knowledge. So for the sake of the Shroud it is proper that we should now try to discover all that can be known about it; and we must be grateful for a book that will tell us with authority how far our learned men have gone on that voyage of discovery.

> The Hon. Sir Steven Runciman

PREFACE

My first contact with Turin and its Shroud came in July 1956 when I arrived in the Piedmontese capital on my way to an ecumenical youth camp in the nearby Waldensian valleys. I remember my first impression of the dark chapel where the Shroud is kept. There was no explanation of what was to be found behind that mysterious-looking grille above the altar but the word *Sindone* figured prominently in the prayer cards and I discovered from my little dictionary that it must be a shroud – the Shroud of Jesus. Growing up in North Carolina as the son and grandson of Lutheran clergymen, my adolescent rebellion had centred in a fascination with exotic facets of Christian tradition. This initial link with the Turin Shroud was to remain largely dormant until twenty years later I started reading everything I could get my hands on concerning this curious object. Father Peter Rinaldi was an early contact and he suggested that I get to know the people in Britain who were involved in studying the Shroud; Dr David Willis, Ian Wilson and Leonard Cheshire were my first encounters. This led to my involvement in the formation of the British Society for the Turin Shroud.

My special interest came to be in the possibility of having the Shroud carbon dated, a pursuit which took me to Turin many times and also gave me the pleasure of getting to know the Shroud's owner, King Umberto II. I never expected to write a book on the subject but the more I studied and learned about the complexities of the Shroud the more I became convinced of the need, that as the research concerning it accelerated, someone 'in the know' should try to set the record straight (as much as it could be!) as to how the cloth came to be tested in 1969–73 and 1978. The politics of the situation fascinated me and I realised that most of the people best qualified to give the full story would not feel free to do so because of attachments and commitments.

Finally I have felt for some time that too much of the writing on the Shroud has been hampered by pet theories such as the attempts to prove that Jesus' 'survival' of the death on the cross is confirmed by the Shroud evidence, or that the Shroud can be given a full historical pedigree from tomb to Turin. I have also been disturbed by some of the overestimation of its religious significance. I have my own biases and suspicions but have tried to keep them to a minimum. I am not a sindonologist – and I've always wondered just how that term was supposed to be used – but I do have a consuming interest in that remarkable piece of linen and have been fortunate enough to have come to know most of the vital people involved with its current study.

I owe a great deal of gratitude to the Reverend Peter Rinaldi, SDB, for making it possible for me to be involved with much of the current research on the Shroud and for his infectious inspiration. He is a polished diplomat and no man has done more than he in making it possible to have the Shroud competently tested and openly studied.

Sir Steven Runciman has been a helpful mentor and wise judge of various aspects of the Shroud's study and I greatly appreciate his many contributions. I would not have dared the undertaking of examining the history of the relic without his valuable assistance.

Dom Sylvester Houédard, OSB, was kind to go through the historical section and make corrections and comments and I only wish that the scope of this volume had been large enough to follow some of his fascinating leads.

Professor Silvio Curto, a member of the 1969 Turin Commission, not only directed me to finding the Raes' samples but offered useful information about the investigations which occurred in Turin in 1969 and 1973.

I also appreciate the advice and information from Dr Robert Bucklin, Dr John Jackson, the Reverend Maurus Green, OSB, Miss Vera Barclay, Don Piero Coero Borga, the Reverend Paul de Gail, SJ, and especially the Rt Revd Dr John A. T. Robinson who has shared so many of his thoughts and wise counsel on the subject.

My associates and students at the American School in London have had to suffer through much of this project and I appreciate their forbearance and good humour. Denise Gregg of the school laboriously and beautifully translated many French sources and Valeria Ossola kindly helped with Italian material.

The study of the Turin Shroud involves an unusual variety of disciplines and it is easy to become entangled with explorations which lead nowhere or cloud central concerns. I have relegated to the chapter notes a few hints which I hope some readers will pursue. I have also taken a basically chronological approach which sometimes means that certain issues have been returned to and Chapter Seven contains material which is of a highly exploratory nature. Here I have especially taken the attitude of letting the information and events 'speak for themselves' and I thank the members of the American team for their many 'breathless' reactions.

CHAPTER I

WHAT IS THE SHROUD OF TURIN?

There are few subjects from the medieval world which evoke more distasteful images in modern minds than do relics – the remains of holy people or objects intimately associated with them. The veneration of relics was practised long before their expressed approval by the Council of Trent at its twenty-fifth session, on 3rd December 1563, which condemned those who held that 'veneration and honour are not due to the relics of the saints'.

The excesses concerning relics bother us; when St Cyprian was about to be beheaded in 258, his devotees cast cloths before him so that these might be soaked in his blood. Centuries later an armed guard spared St Francis' body being carried away from his death bed as a premature relic. In an elegantly bejewelled casket held by two elaborately draped silver gilt angels from the collegiate church of Calcata, north of Rome, are the remains of undoubtedly the most exotic of all relics – the Holy Foreskin, faithfully preserved as the only physical evidence of Jesus Christ on earth.

The vast number of relics assembled by the time of the Protestant Reformation caused John Calvin to remark that if all the fragments of the true cross were brought together, one could build a fleet of ships out of them. There is no doubt that the point of the medieval pilgrimage was to look at relics. A place became a 'tourist resort' in the Middle Ages, when all tourists were pilgrims, not because it had good weather and beaches, but because it had an important relic. It is difficult for us to enter the medieval mind on this subject. We cannot understand what impact such articles as, say, the remains of St Andrew at Vetralla had. But to the devout of the Middle Ages, the fifteenth century silver angel of this reliquary was carefully holding before him a link to Christ. St Andrew had brought his important brother, Peter, to the Lord and the faithful could share in the physical reality of this event, and through the accessible and ordinary Andrew, similarly come to the Lord as well. It was easier to approach the Divine Majesty through such a link.

To us, relics have no such meaning and they received only a scant notice in the documents of the Second Vatican Council: 'The saints have been traditionally honoured in the Church and their authentic relics and images held in veneration. For the feasts of the saints proclaim the wonderful works of Christ in his servants, and display to the faithful fitting examples for their imitation.' That was all the council said. This downplaying of what was once a very elaborate facet of Western Church practice speaks loudly. The post-Vatican II attitude seems to view relics as part of the excess baggage of Christian tradition, easily discarded and forgotten. There is, however, one relic in the Church's treasury not easily discarded or forgotten – one which supersedes all others in interest and potentiality.

Climbing the black marble steps to the Holy Shroud reliquary in the Royal Chapel of Turin Cathedral immediately sets the modern pilgrim in a sombre mood. Entering the chapel you view a large baroque chamber, lofty and oval in form, overlaid with ebony marble. The only relief from the dark atmosphere is the whiteness of the marble tombs of four illustrious princes of Savoy, and a stupendous dome designed by Guarini to give the effect that light is coming from a hidden source. This dominates the Cathedral's unpretentious dome; Guarini's masterpiece is a cupola of intricate geometrical design with six tiers leading to a star-shaped peak, broken by apertures admitting shafts of light to point dramatically to what lies below. Lined with red silk, rolled up in another sheet of silk, the Turin Shroud is in an oblong casket of wrought silver. This is inside an iron chest strengthened by three locks, each of which has a separate key. The iron chest is within a wooden case behind a grille-work, which is all the pilgrim sees above him on a double altar in the centre of the chapel.

The cloth is a yellowish stained linen of fourteen feet, three inches by three feet, seven inches, bearing the front and back imprints of a naked man's body. The linen's colour is like old ivory and the body and the 1,532 burn marks are sepia-coloured, resembling the scorch marks of a well-worn ironing board cover. The texture is surprisingly soft, more like damask than linen, and it is unusually light in weight and supple. The pattern of weaving is clearly herring-bone design, forming somewhat irregular longitudinal bands. It is a three-to-one twill, close and opaque; unbleached and fairly thick thread was used requiring a loom with four pedals.

The impressions of the man's body are on the central portion of the cloth with the front and back head portions near each other but not actually touching. It is as if a body had been sandwiched between the long folded linen. The body images blend into the cloth as if each and every thread were impregnated. In a good light, what appear to be blood marks are of a different hue – a carmine mauve. They stand out subtly from the colour tone of the body, varying slightly according to the wound marks. The body image is in shade and light, without definite boundaries and merging into the background while the blood marks have fairly defined outlines.

The first impression of the face on the cloth is that it adheres well to one's mental picture of Jesus: there is a majesty about it and a certain authority. Second and third looks make it apparent that there is evidence of considerable suffering. Rivulets of blood on frontal and dorsal sides – the most pronounced of which is in the shape of a figure three across the forehead – give the impression that a cap-like structure of spikes had been forced on the head. There seems to be a bruise across the right cheek and the cartilage of the nose appears to be fractured. The short beard is forked and there is a small moustache visible on the upper lip. The long hair seems to stand forward on either side of the face with blank spaces between the sides of the face and the surrounding hair and at the top of the head. There appears to be an unbound 'pigtail' falling to the shoulder-blades of the dorsal image. The absence of a clear neck region gives the head a separated and suspended look.

Contusions are to be found all over the body, most distinctly on the back. They appear as dumb-bell marks, about one and a half inches long, extending from the shoulders down as far as the calves of the legs. On the front of the body they appear on the chest and thighs; on the back they seem to follow a regular pattern: horizontal on the lower back, fanning upwards on the shoulders from either side, downwards on the legs from the right. The back region also has what appears as bruising in the region of the scapulae.

Where the left hand meets the wrist, at the base of the palm, is a vivid mark of blood.[1] The hands are crossed over the groin area, with the left hand on top of the right, covering the right wrist. There are flows of blood on the left and right arms which indicate we are dealing with a crucifixion victim. They follow what would have been the necessary degree angle for crucifixion and also change direction as would be expected.

The feet images are not very distinct on the frontal side but there is an excellent impression of a nearly complete right foot print and the heel of the left foot on the dorsal portion of the cloth. The feet appear to be turned towards each other and are partly crossed left over right. A square image can be seen on the sole of the right foot; a corresponding point is just discernible on the left. From both two separate blood flows emanate.

The thorax is strikingly expanded and there is a fairly large oval wound near the fifth and sixth ribs on the right side from which has flowed blood and a watery fluid. This wound in the side is partly obliterated by one of the triangular-shaped patches which run the length of the cloth on both sides. The only other distinguishing marks are creases, water marks and four curious sets of triple holes in the linen.

We can surmise the following about the man on the Turin Shroud: He was 5ft. 11in. tall (181cm.),[2] weighed approximately 170 pounds and according to the marks left on his burial cloth, he had been beaten more than fifty times with a prong-like object. His head had suffered from a spike-like capping; his face had been struck; he had been crucified through the wrists and feet and his side was punctured.

It was a long time before Christians portrayed their Lord's death by crucifixion. Artistic representations in the catacombs displayed an unwillingness to depict his passion and death. These scenes were not presented in any realistic fashion when they finally appeared. The idea of venerating a figure on a cross was an abomination, something only heathens did to denigrate the followers of Jesus. A graffito on the wall of the pages' room on the Palatine shows a vilifying figure with the head of an ass attached to a cross with the inscription which reads: 'Alexaminos adores his god'. Alexaminos was obviously a young Christian derided by his fellows.

The first crucifixion scenes did not appear until the fifth and sixth centuries, long after Constantine had abolished this form of execution. No artists depicting Jesus' death had witnessed the practice and scanty knowledge was available as to how crucified persons should be portrayed. The British Museum possesses a lovely fifth century ivory box with what may be the earliest surviving representation of Jesus' crucifixion. Here Jesus is lifted up on what appears to be a Tau cross (a vivid 'T' shape) with his arms extended, palms nailed and feet hanging vertically without attachment. Christ is a beardless Apollo; a loin cloth is around his middle and the general effect is of a majestic young god 'standing' in front of his cross against which he extends his arms in triumph.

Perhaps second in age to the British Museum crucifixion scene is a relief from the wooden doors of St Sabina in Rome. Here Jesus is represented in the attitude of prayer like a priest at the altar. The hands of Jesus and the two thieves are not nailed to crosses but to blocks of wood comprising what appears to be a backdrop of three house-like structures outside Jerusalem's walls. Neither of these early portrayals are pictures of a man being put to death and neither has much in common with the relic image in Turin with its portrait of a bloody, naked and bearded victim with the vivid marks of suffering caused by scourging and crucifixion.

CHAPTER 2

WHAT DO THE GOSPELS SAY ABOUT THE SHROUD?

Suppose a forger started creating a replica of Jesus' burial shroud using, as surely he would, the information about the cloth from the gospel accounts. What would he find? First of all it would be difficult for a forger to harmonise some of the material of the four evangelists. These differences have led to various theories of origin, the one which was popular when I was in theological college in the 1950s going as follows; Matthew and Luke include almost the entire content of the less complicated gospel of Mark and they have in common much of what Mark omits. It was deduced that Matthew and Luke must have had access to a source called 'Q' (from the German word for source, *Quelle*). Because of what were called its 'Hellenistic' and 'mystical' qualities, the gospel according to St John was presented in considerable isolation from the others. His tone was different, as one commentator stated, it was 'the spiritual gospel selecting things especially for their spiritual meaning, while the first three give the things obvious to the senses'.[3] This interpretation has been questioned in more recent times. It has been observed that the Aramaic text of Matthew is older than Mark and the seeming simplicity and naïveté of the latter have been overplayed. In his own way, Mark is as concerned as John in presenting a theology of Christ's person, life and work. To some, the gospel of John preserves tradition which carries us back as far as the other evangelists. John's gospel, however, in design and intention, does remain distinct from the three 'synoptic' gospels. The resemblance among the three does allow us to handle them as one unit for certain purposes, as with the passion of Jesus.

None of the gospels are biographies in the modern sense of the term with exact chronology and detailed topography. Despite some popular attempts, it is not possible to reconstruct a detailed 'life of Christ' from the evangelists' accounts. As Father J. Huby has said, '. . . they were primarily occupied in throwing light on the religious values of the life of Christ by a choice of episodes which conveyed his teaching in themselves'. The gospels were never intended to be handled as biography; they are not photographs but rather artistic portraits in the best sense of the term. A photograph shows all; it reproduces the details of the photographed, warts and all. Only occasionally does a photograph give more than a momentary, surface impression of the subject. The great portraits penetrate more deeply than the façade of the portrayed. The gospels are like that. They possess the ability and authenticity to go beneath the surface. Like accomplished portrait artists, the writers of the gospels made full use of the artists' prerogative to arrange the material at hand to emphasise a certain event. In respect to the final days of Jesus' life, those events and details which were remembered as most important to the theme of the Passion, were grouped together. There was no attempt to give the kind of 'eyewitness' reporting, to which we in our day are so accustomed. A forger would have considerable difficulty trying to decide where to begin. Just exactly what should he show – and what would he feel should be eliminated from his presentation of Jesus' death and burial? Let's look at the Gospel evidence. Despite some variances, the first three accounts, the so-called Synoptics, present roughly the following outline of material:

1. On Friday morning, following Jesus' 'trial', Pontius Pilate had him flogged and handed over to be crucified.

2. Jesus was stripped by Pilate's soldiers and dressed in a scarlet mantle.

3. The soldiers plaited a crown of thorns and placed it on his head.

4. Jesus was jeered, spat upon and beaten about the head with a cane.

5. When the soldiers had finished their mockery, Jesus received his own clothing and was led away to be crucified.

6. On the way to the place of execution, Simon of Cyrene was forced to carry Jesus' cross.

7. At the place called the Skull (Golgotha) Jesus was crucified.

8. At about three o'clock, Jesus cried out and was offered a sponge soaked with drugged or sour wine. He again gave a loud cry and died.

9. When evening came on this, the preparation day before the Sabbath, the wealthy disciple and respected member of the council, Joseph of Arimathea, approached Pilate requesting the body. According to Mark, Pilate was surprised that Jesus was already dead but delivered the body to Joseph.

10. Joseph took the body down from the cross, wrapped it in a clean linen cloth *(sindon)* which he bought, and placed it in his own unused tomb which he had cut out of a rock. A large stone was rolled against the entrance. Mary Magdalene and 'the other' Mary were watching and saw where Jesus was placed.

11. On Saturday, at the request of the chief priests and Pharisees (so that the disciples would not steal Jesus' body and claim that he had risen from the dead) a guard was placed at his tomb and it was sealed.

12. Just after sunrise on Sunday morning, after the Sabbath was over, Mary Magdalene and other women went to the tomb with aromatic oils and spices in order to anoint Jesus' body. When they arrived they found that the stone had been rolled away and Jesus was gone.

13. The Authorized Version and other translations add to the Lucan account (since it was part of the original text according to all manuscripts except one) that, after the women reported what they had seen to the apostles, Peter ran to the tomb and, looking in, saw the linen clothes laid by

themselves and he went home 'wondering in himself at that which was come to pass'.

Following the New English Bible, that is substantially the brief outline of events concerning Jesus' death and burial in the Synoptic gospels. Not every detail in this concise outline is repeated in each of the three gospels. John's portrait of the events can be outlined in this manner:

1. On Friday, the eve of Passover, following Jesus' trial Pontius Pilate had him flogged and the soldiers plaited a crown of thorns and placed it on his head and dressed him in a purple cloak. He was mocked and struck on the face.

2. Pilate tried hard to have him released but at last to satisy the crowd, handed him over to be crucified. Jesus, carrying his own cross, went to the Place of the Skull (Golgotha) where they crucified him.

3. When Jesus realized that the end had come, he cried out that he was thirsty.

4. Because it was the eve of Passover, the Jews were anxious that the crucified bodies not remain on the crosses for the coming Sabbath so they requested that the legs be broken (to hasten death) and the bodies taken down. When they came to Jesus, they found that he was already dead so they did not break his legs. One of the soldiers did stab his side with a lance and there was a flow of blood and water.

5. Pilate was approached by Joseph of Arimathea for permission to remove Jesus' body. This was granted and Joseph, joined by Nicodemus, took the body and wrapped it with a mixture of myrrh and aloes in linen clothes (*othonia*) according to Jewish burial practice and placed it in an unused tomb in a garden.

6. Early on Sunday morning, Mary Magdalene came to the tomb and when she saw that the stone had been removed from the entrance, she ran to tell Peter and the other disciple (usually identified as John).

7. Peter and the other disciple ran to the tomb. The latter looked in and saw the linen clothes (*othonia*) but did not enter the tomb. Peter came up behind him and went into the tomb.

He saw the linen clothes and the napkin (*sudarion*), which had been over Jesus' head, not lying with the clothes but rolled together in a place by itself. Then the other disciple went in and saw and believed.

Looking at the markings and images on the Shroud we can see a reconstruction of the Gospel accounts of Jesus' death and burial. The Shroud seems both an independent guide to interpretation and a probing tool for further questioning of these events.

The evidence of some form of flogging is vividly present on the Turin cloth. Scourging had been employed by the Jews from early times but it was only for a very limited number of offences and was handled in a very moderate manner. No more than forty stripes were allowed by Jewish law. Flogging was the normal Roman prelude to capital punishment and the number of stripes and form of instrument were decided by the judge or by the whim of the executioner. Roman legionaries were not known for their restraint. The usual procedure was to strip the prisoner and bind him to a pillar with his arms elevated over his head. Two or three-pronged whips loaded with bone or lead balls were employed. On the dorsal view of the man on the Shroud we find the wounds from the beating have basically the same shape – that of a little halter about three centimetres long. The two circular shapes represent the balls of lead or bone, while the line which joins them is the mark of the thong. Since there are more than one hundred of these, the victim received more than fifty strokes apart from those not leaving the double marks. The imprints seem to be in a sheaf-like fashion directed downward and medially from the shoulders. This could indicate either that two persons were involved in the beating, or that one executioner changed his position from the right to the left side.

St John reports that Jesus was struck in the face. Excoriations are to be found over the facial image of the Shroud, but are more pronounced on the right side. The most noticeable is to be seen on the right cheek joining what is apparently a nasal cartilage abrasion. Perhaps this was created by a cane or stick as suggested in the gospels of Matthew and Mark.

Following the scourging, Jesus was derided by the soldiers by being stripped and having his clothes replaced with the mocking symbols of kingship: a scarlet robe, a reed and a crown of thorns. It has been suggested that this mocking could be connected with the *basileus*, the 'move of the king' which was part of a game like hopscotch called the 'circle game' played by Roman soldiers to relieve the boredom of their jobs. Archaeological discoveries in the courtyard of the Antonia fortress in old Jerusalem have revealed an interesting pavement. Among game markings found with the rough line of a circle are a 'B' for *basileus* and a royal crown. It is not far-fetched to see the scriptural mocking of Jesus as his being chosen as a 'volunteer' king in their sport. The soldiers would revel in having one claimed to be the 'king of the Jews' in their horseplay.

Other scratchings in the Antonia pavement show that the 'crown of thorns' was probably not a plain circlet but had radiating points. The crown indicated by the Turin Shroud is actually a cap-like structure which wounded the whole surface of the cranium. On the dorsal side of the head, one sees flows of blood and wounds on the top and back, explained if the 'cap' were branches and thorns laced over the top of the cap. The face shows several blood prints with one especially vivid mark in the shape of a figure 3. If this cap were on the victim's head during the crucifixion, these marks would have been clearly accentuated by the movement of the head in contact with the cross-beam. The crowning with thorns seems to be a unique detail of Jesus' execution; there are no recorded parallels. Some experts have identified the thorns as the *Paliurus* or *Zizyphus spina* species; these thorns have stipules containing two strong prongs which curve backward and are known to have grown in the neighbourhood of Jerusalem. The damage the crown created especially fascinated Dr Pierre Barbet who made extensive anatomical studies of the Shroud figure in the 1920s and 1930s. He noted how true to life the path of the blood marks on the forehead are: 'following a meandering course obliquely downwards and outwards . . . broadening progressively just as a flow of blood does on a wounded man when it meets obstacles'.

The 'Crown of Thorns' was the prized relic purchased by St Louis in 1239 from Venetian merchants who had brought it from Constantinople. Paris' elegant Sainte Chapelle was built to house it. In its crystal case it is today in Notre Dame, a crown without any thorns. The relic is a circlet of plaited rushes and some writers have speculated that in relationship to the Shroud's evidence, it would appear that after the soldiers had imposed thorns upon Jesus' head, they fixed it securely with this circlet, binding it all around the head.

St John's gospel does not indicate that Simon of Cyrene was pressed into service to carry Jesus' cross but says that Jesus 'was carrying his own cross . . . to the Place of the Skull'. Some see that there are a mass of excoriations in the region of the shoulder blades, suggesting the weight and friction of what might have been a rough beam, carried at least part of the route to the place of execution. It is generally agreed that what was carried was the moveable crossbeam, the *patibulum*, not the entire cross which would have weighed more than three hundred pounds.

Cicero called crucifixion 'the most cruel and frightful of all forms of death'. It is thought to have originated in the East and is known to have been practised by the Persians and the Phoenicians and was introduced into the Greco-Roman world at an early stage, certainly reaching Rome by the time of Tarquinius Superbus. The Romans confined this execution almost exclusively to slaves, foreigners and criminals of the lowest class; it was seen as incompatible with the dignity of Roman citizens (Paul being a citizen was exempt from the possibility – Peter is said to have died in this manner). It was an intentionally degrading death.

The procedure of crucifixion varied according to circumstances, but usually, after the victim was stripped of all his clothing and scourged, he was laid on the ground while his outstretched arms were fixed to the *patibulum* by ropes or nails. The cross beam was then lifted up with the body on it and fixed on the top of the *stipes*, the upright beam, as a 'T' or across it as a '†'. The feet were then fastened with either thongs or nails.

Certainly one of the most telling features of the Shroud image is the marking of nail wounds in the wrist rather than the palm region as depicted in traditional art.[4] The trickles of blood on both forearms suggest that the arms were raised well above the head, supporting the weight of the body. Medical experts have stated many times that it would be impossible for the palm region to support such weight; but there are at least two areas in the wrist–forearm region which could do so: the Destot space which was favoured by Pierre Barbet and the space between the radius and the ulna which has been suggested by Dr Anthony Sava. There is no disagreement that the Shroud picture indicates that the left foot was nailed over the right one with one nail piercing both feet.

Roman crucifixion combined extreme bodily pain, with the tortures of hunger, thirst, heat and insects, all suffered while the naked victim's bodily functions were beyond his control. Fastened to the wood, the body contracted in spasms with wounds swelling, and lungs and heart congested to breaking point. Death might not follow for many hours, and some victims lasted for several days. Dr Barbet assumed that because of the position of the man on the cross, suspended by nails in his outstretched wrists with no other support than the nailed feet, he must have died of asphyxia – slowly choking to death. This he claimed, was induced by muscular spasm and fixation of the chest in breathing. Some years ago, Dr Hermann Mödder of Cologne carried out scientific experiments to ascertain the cause of Jesus' death. Mödder used medical students to discover that when a person is suspended by his two hands the blood sinks very quickly to the lower half of the body. After six to twelve minutes blood pressure has dropped by fifty per cent, and the pulse rate has doubled. Too little blood reaches the heart and fainting ensues. This leads to a speedy orthostatic collapse through insufficient blood circulating to the brain and heart and that was the cause of death. This point will be discussed in Chapter Five.

The Romans had a sure way of bringing about death for crucified victims – the *crurifragium* when the legs were broken below the knee with blows from a club. Often on the *stipes* there was a small support called a *sedile* (seat), or sometimes there was a foot-rest. If the victim eased his misery from time to time by supporting himself on either of these, the blood returned to the upper half of his body and the faintness passed. With the *crurifragium*, this support was gone and death followed more easily. The Jews were anxious not to have the crucified bodies remaining on their crosses over the Sabbath[5] and, in John's gospel, they asked Pilate to have the legs broken. After doing this to those who were crucified with Jesus, they discovered that the Nazarene was already dead so there was no need to break his legs.

One of the soldiers did pierce his side with a spear[6] and, according to St John, 'at once there came out blood and water'. In the view of some medical experts, the very clear 'spear wound' in the side is the most interesting of all the Shroud markings as far as medical evidence is concerned. It has some strange characteristics: there are white patches throughout its dimensions and the edge has a scalloped shape in places. Dr Barbet ascertained that the lance penetrated between the fifth and sixth rib on the right side, boring through the right lung, perforating the pericardium and piercing the right auricle of the heart. The 'water' then would be the clear fluid of the pericardial sac. Dr Anthony Sava has stated that this fluid is so small in amount that it would be hardly noticed. Writing in the *Catholic Biblical Quarterly* he explained:

> The Gospel gives a clear impression that no time elapsed between the piercing of the side and the gush of blood. One might be justified in suspecting that an accumulation of blood and water was immediately inside the rib cage waiting to be evacuated . . . Experience with severe chest injuries has demonstrated that non-penetrating injuries of the chest are capable of producing an accumulation of haemorrhagic fluid in the pleural cavity. It may amount to

as much as three pints . . . The red blood cells tend to gravitate towards the bottom, while the lighter clearer serum accumulates in the upper half of the collection as a separate contiguous layer . . . I submit . . . that the brutal scourging of Christ several hours before . . . death . . . was sufficient to produce a bloody accumulation within the chest so that the settling by this fluid into layers and its ultimate evacuation by opening the chest below the level of separation must inevitably result in the immediate flow of blood and water in that order.[7]

(We return to this discussion in Chapter Five).

Sava has pointed out the underestimated importance of Jesus' scourging which others have also stressed, including Dr Christopher McManus of Oxford's Psychological Laboratory who has called it 'the first pathological event'. This brutal punishment would have had all sorts of consequences: loss of blood, removal of a large amount of skin with the attendant bodily fluid loss and, as Dr McManus has pointed out, due to the large amount of blood clotting in the body, it would gradually use up resources for future clotting and the victim would just bleed. It is therefore not necessary to see the spear piercing the heart as so important – 'there were enough other reasons for Jesus to die' as McManus has put it.

Mary Magdalene and Mary the mother of Joseph . . . saw where he was laid. (Mark)

Mary Magdalene was there, and the other Mary, sitting opposite the grave. (Matthew).

The women . . . took note of the tomb and observed how his body was laid. (Luke).

The Synoptic gospels absolutely insist that the tomb found empty on Sunday morning was the one in which Jesus' body had been placed on the previous Friday. According to their accounts, the women did not go to the wrong grave because having followed Joseph of Arimathea they knew the site of burial. When they got there they faced what Jewish scholar, Geza Vermes, has called 'the one disconcerting fact' which must be faced by all interpreters, 'namely that the women who set out to pay their respects to Jesus found, to their consternation, not a body but an empty tomb'.[8]

There was one person who could not leave that tomb. Mary Magdalene, having told Peter and John that the stone had been removed from the entrance, returned to the tomb and stayed there. Even though she thought that he had been taken away it was there she wished to be. This was the place of latest association with him and she would stay.

Mary's reaction that 'they have taken the Lord out of his tomb and we do not know where they have laid him' is followed by that of 'John'. He noticed both the linen clothes and the 'napkin' still lying in the tomb. It must have seemed inconceivable that anyone stealing the corpse would have left the linen clothes in such a fashion – with the 'napkin' which had been over (or around) Jesus' head rolled together in a place by itself. Something of an entirely different nature must have occurred. 'The other disciple' now grasped the meaning of the puzzling discovery and we are told 'he saw and believed'. Peter first looked into the tomb but did not see the significance. However, in Luke's added account, he 'went home wondering at that which was come to pass'.

What they saw is a complicated matter of interpretation and commentators have varied in their analyses. The Jews had neither 'undertakers' nor formal cemeteries during the time of Jesus. Family or friends would wash a body and anoint it with oils and spices. In the absence of relatives or friends, it was a work of merit to arrange for the burial of a body by a pious Jew. Jewish custom insisted on prompt burial as a matter of respect for the dead and a necessity in a hot climate. Writing in his *Jewish Wars*, Josephus noted that even crucified criminals were taken down and buried before sunset. The most typical choice of tomb was a natural cave or chamber cut into soft rock. Bodies were placed in recesses or on shelves or slabs of stone and the entrance was closed either with a rounded stone fitted in a groove which could be rolled back if necessary, but was also too heavy to be casually tampered with.[9] The dead person was laid on his back, having been ceremoniously washed by more than one person.[10] According to an article by A. P. Bender in the *Jewish Quarterly Review*, 'the dead must likewise not be moved from one position to another by fewer than two persons. The corpse is first laid on a deal board, with its feet turned towards the door, and covered with a clean sheet . . . It was formerly the custom also to anoint the corpse with aromatic spices . . . The custom of actual embalming, as understood by the Egyptians, does not seem to have found favour with the Jews, as instances of the practice are extremely rare in the history of Israel.'[11]

A mummy-type burial with strips of linen wrapped round the body was not part of Jewish burial custom. Unlike the Egyptians, the Jews were not interested in preserving the bodies of the dead in their present physical form. From the evidence we have, they buried their dead in shrouds and left them to decay in the tomb. The Synoptic gospels mention a *sindon*, a shroud, as having wrapped or enfolded the body of Jesus. The Turin Shroud has no difficulty corresponding to this, and is similar to the 'grave-vestments' mentioned in Bender's article:

> . . . They (the grave-vestments in the Mishnah) are identical with the sindon of the New Testament . . . being made of white linen without the slightest ornament, and must be stainless. They are usually the work of women, and are simply pieced together, no knots being permitted, according to some, in token that the mind of the dead is disentangled of the cares of this life, but in the opinion of others, as representing the expression of a wish that the bones of the dead may be speedily dissolved into their primitive dust.[12]

St John's gospel has words describing the burial clothes which some have seen as incompatible with the foregoing. 'They took the body of Jesus and wrapped it, with the spices, in strips of linen cloth *(othonia)* according to Jewish burial-customs.' This is how The New English Bible interprets John 19.40. The Authorized Version had used the words, '. . . and wound it in linen clothes . . .' The NEB goes on to read: 'Then Simon Peter came up . . . and he went into the tomb. He saw the linen wrappings *(othonia)* lying, and the napkin *(sudarion)* which had been over his head, not lying with wrappings *(othonia)* but rolled together in a place by itself.' (John 20.6–7). The Authorized Version called the *othonia* 'linen clothes' and the *sudarion*, 'the napkin'. The interpretation of the *othonia* as 'strips of linen' is a fairly modern one and reflects later assumptions. Having Jesus bound with linen strips in an Egyptian fashion is against Jewish custom as we have seen and also there would have been no time in the necessarily hurried and temporary burial for such an elaborate procedure to be performed. Use of binding strips over the usual burial linen would have been placed very loosely in anticipation of the final burial when the Sabbath had passed. The Greek term, *othonia*, means 'linens' and in the judgment of John A. T. Robinson and others it is referring to 'clothes' – it need not even mean *grave* clothes. It is a pity that John was not more explicit in his choice of words but there is no difficulty in the Shroud being included in such a general term as the Greek *othonia*. Of this Dr Robinson has said: 'John speaks of (the body) being bound (or, according to one manuscript, wrapped) in *othonia*. Luke (24.12), if it is part of his text, as I believe it is, uses the word in his resurrection story for what he has previously described as the *sindon*.'[13]

Some interpreters have insisted that the *sudarion* was not a veil or napkin-like article but the shroud itself.[14] The reason for this view is their wanting to make certain they had a linen which clearly went over the face and head, as well as the body.[15] One still finds the shroud called a *sudarion* in Spanish and other accounts. The etymological difficulty with this view is that it is improbable that the Greek word sudarion would mean anything large enough to cover the length of a man twice. *Sudarion* is a 'loan word' from Latin defining a cloth object not by its material but by its function; to wipe away sweat. The word designated what we would call a handkerchief, as with that of the servant in Luke 19.20 who kept the pound his master had given him.

Dr Robinson with other New Testament scholars had identified the *sudarion* as a jaw-band:

> John specifies also a sudarion or sweat-cloth, which he says was tied 'round the face' of Lazarus and 'went over the head' of Jesus. If, as we must assume, this refers to the same burial practice, the only position that fits both descriptions is of something passing crossways over the head, round the face and under the chin. In other words it describes a jaw-band, made evidently by folding or rolling diagonally a large handkerchief or neckerchief, rather like our triangular bandage. This would have been functionally necessary to hold the mouth shut before *rigor mortis* set in, and which the Mishnah specifically refers to as being allowable to tie on the Sabbath, providing the jaw was not moved. This interpretation of the sudarion is accepted by a number of commentators, including the late Joe Sanders of Cambridge, on the New Testament evidence alone, and seems to me well-nigh certain.

The custom of placing aromatic spices with Jewish corpses is well substantiated but the vast quantity mentioned in John's account has troubled some writers – 'one hundred pounds' – which would be equivalent to sixty-seven pounds today. Perhaps this was 'a rich man's tribute' not unlike the kind of tribute paid to the living in Jesus' day when ointments were poured over the heads of honoured guests at a banquet. This, of course, reminds us of Mary Magdalene's anointing of Jesus, of which he said, 'She has anointed my body beforehand to prepare it for burial.' Nicodemus' 'mixture of myrrh and aloes' was not for elaborate embalming as in Egyptian usage but was probably laid in the tomb beside the body. Some have suggested that it had been packed round the sides of the body giving an explanation for the relatively flat lying of the Shroud and the lack of distortion, as indicated by the photographed images.

There have been a number of interpretations in Biblical commentaries as to what Peter and the 'other disciple' witnessed in John's account of the empty tomb. Some have given the view that Jesus passed through the linen clothes and *sudarion* 'like a sun through a window pane'. This was a logical conclusion to the resurrection appearances which followed, where Jesus passed through material objects such as the door of the upper room. A dematerialisation was clearly implied to writers like Wilbert F. Howard in The Interpreter's Bible:

> The explanation that best fits the Johannine view of the mode of the Resurrection is that the body had been swiftly dematerialised, leaving the swathing clothes as they were . . . if the body of Jesus had been carried away from the tomb, either the grave clothes would have been taken away with the body, or else they would have been scattered on the floor of the sepulchre. It was their position that made the disciple leap to the conclusion that the material body had been transformed into a spiritual body.

Though this explanation seems a fairly reasonable assessment of the words John uses, it is difficult to see dematerialisation as being the way a Jew at the time of Jesus would interpret life after death.[16] Christians are surprised to discover that Jews of the first century did not have a precise doctrine of the hereafter (as is still the case). Unlike their Greek and Egyptian neighbours, the Jews did not develop a general belief in immortality. The oldest view to be found in the Torah was that death was the final end. Nothing followed when the *rouach*, the 'breath of life' was gone. There were mentionings of a strange shadowy domain known as *Sheol* in some Old Testament writings, 'a place of darkness and of the shades of death' in Job. This was vastly different from the land of the living.

By the time of Jesus, some Jews like the Pharisees were beginning to accept the idea that the bodies of the dead would live again although the Sadducees and Samaritans rejected this since it was not to be found in the Pentateuch. The idea of resurrection was speculated by many ordinary people in Palestine and some sectarian groups, but it would be Jesus' own teachings and act of rising from the dead which would bring the idea into unparalleled prominence among religionists in his homeland.

Dr Robinson's suggestion of 'transmaterialisation' seems to fit the circumstances best. As he has stated this is the realm of angelic messengers; bodies of 'glory', 'light' and 'spirit' perceived through the eyes of faith and vision. Jesus' transfiguration is of this order: '. . . he was transfigured; his face shone like the sun, and his clothes became white as the light.' (Matthew 17.2).[17] A similar description is given of the 'angel of the Lord' at the tomb: 'His face shone like lightning; his garments were white as snow. At the sight of him the guards shook with fear and lay like the dead.' (Matthew 28.3–4). In the Old Testament we have the picture of Moses coming down from Mt Sinai: 'When Aaron and the Israelites saw how the skin of Moses' face shone, they were afraid to approach him . . .' (Exodus 34.30). His countenance was so brilliant that he had to wear a veil when he addressed his people.

Writing in 1940, Col P. W. O'Gorman had some fascinating insights into the possible image creation process of the Turin Shroud – particularly considering that the author's conclusions, in part, were so near to scientific views expressed thirty years later. O'Gorman speculated that the images were caused by a photographic-type process or some form of radiation. Relating this to 'miraculous or semi-miraculous' dimensions he wrote:

> In our Lord's case it is suggested that the radiation occurring at the earliest, just immediately before his complete revivication and therefore somewhat moderate in intensity, caused the impression of the body on the sensitised Shroud, the variation in shading being due to the blood, sweat, hair, features, and other usual obstructions to light, as in an ordinary photograph. Instantly on revivication the Shroud was cast aside, and this would account for the impression being of the *dead* Christ and not of the risen Christ, with eyes open, etc.[18]

It has become apparent to some involved with interpreting the Shroud evidence that we should take a serious look at the realm of paranormal physics and psychology, a shadowy domain studded with sometimes questionable vested interests and only marginally accepted in academic circles. Charles Dickens in *Bleak House* gave an account of what he called 'Spontaneous Combustion' of one of his characters, Mr Krook. Dickens stated in his preface to the first edition that this episode was based on investigations into the subject and that thirty cases of this phenomenon had been recorded. There are those in the field of parapsychology who speak of man having an 'astral' or 'etheric' dimension in addition to the physical body. Numerous cases of 'out of the body' experiences have been presented and seen as 'foretastes' of what occurs at death.

Two Englishmen writing recently to the *Sunday Times* suggested the following:

> The intensity of Jesus' intellectual and imaginative perception evidenced by the folklore of his life, suggests to us that he was a very powerful medium. We have heard first-hand accounts of the capacity of some mediums to relay psychic impressions of other people, living or dead, in the form of photographs. Perhaps if there was no other psychic force involved then, under conditions of intense, trance-like suspension, an ego-transmission surely becomes a possibility? But a transmission needs a receiver, just as a normal medium in those circumstances needs an audience, or a photographic plate. Suppose the bromides and nitrates present in the cloth and in the 100 lb. of 'spices' brought by Joseph of Arimathea, produced exactly that condition in the shroud. Might we not expect the earliest known photographic image?

Probably more to the point of the Shroud evidence are the accounts of Buddhist holy men who quite literally were 'absorbed into light'. Chogyam Trungpa in his *Born in Tibet*, wrote:

> We had been told the story of a very saintly man who had died there the previous year . . . Just before his death the

old man said, 'When I die you must not move my body for a week; that is all I desire.'[19] They wrapped his dead body in old clothes and called in lamas and monks to recite and chant. The body was carried into a small room, little bigger than a cupboard, and it was noted that though the old man had been tall the body appeared to have become smaller . . . On the sixth day on looking into the room the family saw it had grown still smaller. A funeral service was arranged for the morning on the eighth day and men came to take the body to the cemetery; when they undid the coverings there was nothing inside except nails and hair. The villagers were astounded, for it would have been impossible for anyone to have come into the room, the door was always kept locked and the window of the little resting place was much too small. (It was later discovered) that such a happening had been reported several times in the past . . . (and it was believed) that the body of the saintly man had been absorbed into the Light . . .[20]

From the angelic account that 'He is not here' to the numerous psychic experiences of our day we are carried into a realm of thinking and study difficult to chart or comprehend. One thing is certain, questions raised by paranormal psychic phenomena have been taken far more seriously in the past few years than anyone would have dared prognosticate when we were all younger and far more sceptical. This is a sphere which will be important in future discussions of the implications of the Turin Shroud evidence.

Discussions of the gospel accounts of Jesus' death, burial and grave clothes indicate that though there are some difficulties, it can be said that there is nothing in the Bible which overrules the possible identification of the Turin Shroud with the shroud of the New Testament. On the contrary, examinations of the original meanings of the words used for the grave garments, the Jewish burial customs involved and the historical practice of crucifixion all tend to indicate that it could be a genuine article. The Turin Shroud's historical pedigree is a much thornier matter.

CHAPTER 3

WHAT IS THE SHROUD'S HISTORY?

It is a peculiar irony that the Turin Shroud's strongest case for authenticity is in the realm of science and its weakest is in its history. Even compiling a brief and accurate account of its indisputable history is not an easy task – certainly not as easy as some authors have made it appear. The novice to Shroud studies becomes easily frustrated in his attempts to find a clear and concise assessment of the known facts. Any lecturer on the Shroud knows how difficult it is to answer the well-intentioned query: 'Just what is the cloth's history?' Many who become excited about the scientific statements expressed about its unique image assume that a fully documented history of the Shroud from the tomb to Turin must exist, and at least one modern writer has tried to supply just that.

Most historians of the Shroud agree that the undisputed history of the Turin relic begins in France with Geoffrey I de Charny between 1353 and 1356. Between those years, records indicate that Geoffrey, seigneur of Lirey (near Troyes) placed it in the church he had wished to build in that district. How he came to possess it is not known although, as we shall see, his son stated that it was a 'gift' and his granddaughter Margaret said it was a *butin de guerre* (spoil of war). Some writers have insisted that King Philip VI had given it to Geoffrey 'for his services'. This is supported by the historical note on the college of Lirey to be found in the Bibliothèque de Paris. There are no documents to support the frequently repeated statement that the church at Lirey was 'founded for the purpose of housing the Shroud'. When Charles Avery,

Deputy Keeper of the Victoria and Albert Museum wrote his brochure on the Lirey reredos, he came across no mention whatsoever of the Shroud in the Lirey district records.[21] We do know from a decree by the Avignon Pope Clement VII in 1390 that the Shroud was 'reverently placed' by Geoffrey I de Charny in Lirey. His small wooden church was dedicated to the Annunciation in 1353 and was a *collegiale* (a collegiate church endowed for canons) established under the aegis of the Troyes diocese. From some accounts, Geoffrey was the knightly ideal – 'generous in combat, open-minded, a writer of verse, a man of great integrity and piety.'[22] He died at the Battle of Poitiers, the Royal Banner of France in his hand, defending with his own body the King, John the Good, who was captured by the Black Prince. The secret of Geoffrey's acquiring the Shroud died with him.

In 1389, Geoffrey's son obtained permission from Pierre, Cardinal de Thury, the Papal Legate, to exhibit the relic. Apparently he did not want to go through all the red tape of asking every local bishop for this permission and the local bishop of Troyes, Pierre d'Arcis, was not pleased about this possible 'slight' to his authority, especially considering the popularity of the expositions in his diocese. The bishop approached the Pope directly. In his communication (we have only the draft of the letter), d'Arcis told Clement VII that his predecessor, Henri de Poitiers, after 'diligent inquiry and examination' had declared the Lirey cloth to be 'cunningly painted – the truth being attested by the artist who painted it'. The bishop did not want to have his flock misled by this spurious relic and demanded that the ostentation be stopped. Clement VII responded by allowing the expositions to continue with the understanding that the Lirey priests clearly state to all that the relic was a 'representation' of Jesus' shroud and he also insisted that the bishop keep *perpetuum silentium* over the matter. This ended the affair but the d'Arcis memorandum would become the chief ammunition of the influential critic of the Shroud in the late nineteenth century, Canon Ulysse Chevalier. D'Arcis died in 1395, leaving no further evidence about his notion that the relic was a forgery. This memorandum is the only source that an investigation was made by d'Arcis' predecessor and that there had been an admission as to its being a painted forgery.

Geoffrey II de Charny began to exhibit the Shroud under the conditions stated by the Pope and the cloth again was an object of pilgrimage. It was displayed to the faithful with no ecclesiastical objection. A badge *(mereau)* worn by medieval pilgrims was found in the mud of the Seine river bed in 1855 which referred to the expositions of the Lirey shroud. The arms of the de Charnys and the Vergys (the family of Geoffrey I's wife) can be seen with the frontal and dorsal images of the relic, over the empty tomb. There can be little doubt that the de Charny relic was one of the more important objects of devotion in France during the latter part of the fourteenth century. Geoffrey II de Charny died in 1398 and item 3898 in the collection of burial effigies compiled by Roger de Gaignieres recorded 'l'effigie d'un chevalier dans un encadrement gothique. Tire de l'abbaye be Froidmont.' (The effigy of a knight under Gothic canopy in the abbey of Froidment). His daughter, Margaret, married Humbert, count of La Roche, who became the new lord of Lirey.[23] Geoffrey II had returned the Shroud to the Lirey canons but fighting was near at hand and the canons decided that not only the Shroud but all their relics would be safer in the hands of the Lirey lord. Count Humbert died in 1438, without a direct heir and without returning the relics. The lands were bequeathed to his nephew, Francois de la Palud, and his widow was made trustee of the Shroud. So jealously did she guard her possession that it went with her on her many travels. The canons at Lirey felt that the times were peaceful enough to have the relic returned, and to ensure this, they were obliged to summon her before the court of Dole. Margaret was willing to part with all the relics save the Shroud which she considered should stay in the custody of the family, having been received by her grandfather as a gift in recognition of war services. Furthermore, she did not feel it would be safe in Lirey. The court of Dole permitted her to keep the Shroud until 1446 and this expiry date was later lengthened to 1449 and again 1452 by other officials. Margaret had expositions of the relic in the diocese of Liège and on one occasion the bishop of the area asked for the credentials of the cloth. All she could present was, of course, the bull of Pope Clement VII which included the statement that the relic was to be displayed as a 'representation' of Christ's shroud. Two ecclesiastics who had been asked to investigate the matter viewed the cloth as *miro artifico depicta* (depicted beautifully and wonderfully). When the final expiry date arrived, Margaret had become as attached to the curious article as her grandfather and she refused to surrender it.

How the Shroud left Margaret's hands and ended in the custody of the House of Savoy is one of those complicated historical situations not easily summarised. There are several interesting people who must be taken into account in what transpired. First of all, there was the strong-willed Margaret, probably in financial difficulties at the time; then the Lirey canons, who remained as determined as ever to retrieve the Shroud; and Humbert's heir, a figure 'who liked to battle, fight and seek quarrels'. In one of these he lost his nose which was replaced by one of silver. He also stormed and sacked the city of Trevoux on the Saône which roused the ire of the Duke of Savoy. The Duke was at first reluctant to deal with him, but eventually at the urging of his wife, the beautiful and abrasive Anne of Cyprus, he banished La Palud from Savoy and confiscated his possessions. The Duke was at the same time having his difficulties with King Charles VII and at this point Margaret emerged asking for compensation for what had been taken from her nephew. Through this clouded situation the Holy Shroud of Lirey passed to the House of Savoy which remains the legitimate owner to this day. It was well known that the Duke's wife had expressed an interest in it, and had asked for it on at least one occasion. Despite all the claims of the Lirey chapter, the cloth became a possession of the House of Savoy on 22 March 1453. There is one charming, surely apocryphal, account presented by the sixteenth century historian, Pignone, that Margaret gave the cloth to

Duke Louis because when she was returning to Burgundy the relic-bearing mule stopped at the gate of Chambery and refused to budge. She interpreted this as a sign that the Duke's (or more exactly his wife's) known desire to have the relic should be heeded. Margaret did not profit from the exchange. The revenues of the fief Miribel granted to her were already exhausted. In spite of a sentence of excommunication for Margaret obtained by the Lirey canons from the ecclesiastical judge of Besançon, they pursued her without result. She died in 1460, followed by the Duke in 1465 and finally his widow, and the promised money compensation to the Lirey church was never paid.

With the Shroud as Savoyard property, we enter a quieter and less complicated era of the cloth's history. Instead of assertions that the cloth was a painted copy and ecclesiastical attempts to stop expositions, we enter a time of veneration by several saints and honours granted by the Holy See. When a special collegiate church was established at Chambery by the Duke of Savoy in 1456, Pope Sixtus IV bestowed upon it the title of Sainte Chapelle (like its more famous forebear in Paris). Pope Julius II initiated a special mass and office of the Holy Shroud for Chambery; Leo X extended the privilege to all of Savoy.

The days at Chambery were fairly quiet, uneventful ones and we possess some interesting accounts of the relic being viewed there by travellers. The 1517 travel diary of Don Antonio de Beatis, companion of the Cardinal Archbishop of Aragon relates the following impressions of the cloth:

> This winding-sheet, sindon or sudarion, is about five and a half spans high and only a little longer than the imprint, which is double – a front and a rear impression. These images of the most glorious body are impressed and shaded in the most precious blood of Jesus Christ and show most distinctly the marks of the scourging, of the cords about the hands, of the crown on the head, of the wounds to the hands and the feet, and especially of the wound in the most holy side, as well as various drops of blood spilled outside

the most sacred image – all in a manner that would strike terror and reverence into Turks, let alone Christians.

Antoine Lalaing, a companion of the French prince, Philippe de Beau, mentions that during a series of expositions the relic underwent some strange tests for authenticity, including its being boiled in oil, but the testers found it impossible to remove the markings. Ian Wilson has suggested that the curious four sets of triple holes in the linen (certainly identified as early as 1516 on a painted copy) may have been created by a red-hot poker in a 'trial by fire' ceremony. There is no record of this but it is an interesting conjecture.

The Shroud attracted the attention of the reformer, John Calvin, who went to see it out of curiosity and rejected it as genuine on the grounds that it was not mentioned in the Scriptures. The most important event in the relic's stay at Chambery occurred on 4th December 1532 when fire broke out in the sacristy of the Sainte Chapelle. Within minutes the entire building was in flames and so intense did the fire become that the silver casket containing the Shroud began to melt. Two laymen and two Franciscan priests risked their lives in the burning building rescuing the cloth. Drops of molten silver had fallen on the linen and burned through its forty-eight layers but the image was almost entirely missed. The scars on the edges of the cloth are to this day the first thing noticed when the Shroud is viewed. The order of Poor Clares repaired the scorched places with triangular-shaped patches of altar linen and left a vivid description of the cloth. The sisters especially noted that, judging from the marks it made, the crown of thorns was more like a cap than its conventional portrayal.[24]

Increasingly in the sixteenth century, the Italian side of the Savoy duchy came to be the centre of concern and there was a disposal of possessions on the French slopes of the Alps. Turin was to be the new Savoyard capital and it was natural that the prized relic should be taken there in 1578. There was a more immediate reason for its being in Turin: Charles

Borromeo, Archbishop of Milan, had vowed to walk to the Chambery shrine if his city were spared the plague. Duke Emmanuel Philibert decided to spare Borromeo the arduous journey by bringing the relic to Turin. On Holy Cross Day, 14 September 1578, the procession entered the capital. The cloth was carried by five bishops and the Duke. The Papal Nuncio and Venetian Ambassador were present with a bevy of other dignitaries. The Shroud was henceforth linked with important events in the House of Savoy. The last three expositions were held in 1898, 1931 and 1933. The 1898 exposition was marked by the extraordinary results of photographing the cloth, to be discussed in Chapter Five. That event started the scientific examination of the Shroud.[25]

The foregoing is a short summary of the fairly reliable history of the Turin Shroud. If that portion of its history was sometimes difficult to pinpoint, the earlier years present an even more formidable problem. Outside the Gospels, the oldest reference to the shroud of Jesus is found in the apocryphal Gospel to the Hebrews. As St Jerome quoted it: 'Now the Lord, when he had given the shroud to the servant of the priest, went to James and appeared to him. For James had taken an oath that he would not eat bread from that hour on which he had drunk the cup of the Lord, till he saw him risen from the dead.'

C. H. Dodd, in *The Commonweal* (October 1931) conjectured that the original reading was Simon (Peter) instead of servant, and he points to the shorter ending of Mark in the *Codex Bobbiensis*, where there is a Latin reading *puero* (servant) in mistake for *Petro* (Peter). Hugh Schonfield writing about this text in 1932 said:

It is . . . likely that the original did state that Jesus gave the shroud to Peter, because Paul among the appearances of the risen Christ mentions the appearance to James but states that 'he was first seen of Cephas (Peter)' (I Corinthians 15.5). Luke, together with John, records the finding of the grave-clothes in the tomb by Peter, and he evidently knew that Peter had seen Jesus, for he makes the eleven say to the two disciples who had returned from Emmaus, 'The Lord is risen indeed, and hath appeared to Simon' (Luke, 24.34).[26]

St Nino, the fourth century apostle of Georgia, also has an account of Peter's possession of the Lord's shroud as does the Syrian, Ishodad of Merv. The latter, writing in 850 said that the burial linens were given to Joseph of Arimathea, but the shroud was taken by Simon Peter and remained with him.

There are also other scattered mentions of Jesus' shroud in the early centuries of the Christian era. St Braulion, the bishop of Saragossa, visited the Holy Land and wrote in 631 of the 'winding sheet in which the body of the Lord was wrapped' and concluded by saying, 'The Scriptures do not tell us that it was preserved, but one cannot call those superstitious who believe in the authenticity of this winding-sheet.' Another visitor to the holy places, Arculph, a French bishop, related how as a pilgrim he had seen and kissed the *Sudarium Domini*. Arculph was shipwrecked off the coast of Scotland and recalled his experiences at the Iona monastery in *c*. 670. Other references can be found in the writings of St John Damascene, the Venerable Bede, St Willibald, Peter the Deacon and William of Tyre. It is from the last named source that we get evidence that the Shroud was in Constantinople by at least the thirteenth century. Since the time of St Helen and Constantine, many of the important relics of Christendom were finding their way to the New Rome. William of Tyre was born in Jerusalem of a French family who had gone there during the Crusades. A learned ecclesiastic, William was canon of Tyre and tutor to the young Baldwin IV of Jerusalem. He recorded seeing in one of the sacred rooms of Constantinople 'the nails, lance, sponge, crown of thorns and sydoine in which the Saviour was wrapped'. This was during an official visit to the Emperor.

We tread on even firmer ground with an account by Robert de Clari, one of the chroniclers of the Fourth Crusade. When it comes to describing events which he witnessed himself or actions in which he took part, he is a vivid and fascinating source of information. De Clari was a knight from Picardy and acted like a medieval war reporter, having an incredible curiosity about everything he saw in Constantinople. One of the things he saw sounded very much like the Shroud as we know it: 'And among these others, there was another of the monasteries which was called Our Lady Saint Mary of Blachernae, where was the shroud *(li sydoines)*, in which our Lord was wrapped, which was stretched up every Friday, so that one could well see on it the figure of our Lord . . .'[27]

In 1210, Nicolas Mesarites defended the relics of the Bucoleon chapel against a mob and in a dramatic speech he pointed to the sacred place and declared, 'In this temple Christ rises again, and the shroud with the burial linens are the clear proof'. In an inventory of relics in the Grand Palace, he described the sepulchral linens of Jesus 'still smelling of myrrh, defying destruction, having enveloped the mysterious, naked dead body after the Passion'. The two words, 'mysterious' and 'naked' according to the Benedictine, Maurus Green, 'suggest that he knew more than he told the mob'.

There is therefore a fairly reliable account of a shroud similar to the Turin relic being kept in Constantinople in the thirteenth century. This important link in the Shroud's history disappeared as dramatically as it had appeared. De Clari reported 'nobody knew, neither Greek nor Frank, what became of this shroud when the town was taken'.[28] 'When the town was taken' was one of the greatest blots of medieval history – the fourth crusade. It had been arranged in 1199 by Count Thibaut III of Champagne and other French nobles and blessed by Pope Innocent III with transportation provided by Enrico Dandolo, the doge of Venice. Lacking the necessary passage money when they assembled at Venice, the French crusaders were forced to accept the Venetian plan to capture and sack the Christian city of Zara. This was followed by further Venetian trickery which ended in the conquest and merciless pillage of the Byzantine capital. For the first time in 900 years, Constantinople was stormed and occupied by a foreign force. The God-guarded walls had failed it; the sacred icons and innumerable relics had not been able to protect it. Realizing that they would not be fighting 'the infidel', the only thing that seemed to hold this Christian army together was the prospect of loot. Recognising that churches would contain the best and most accessible riches many crusaders went immediately to the great temples of worship, including the chief prize, Santa Sophia, where in the course of pillaging they desecrated everything held sacred by the Byzantines. They got drunk from communion wine, and raped and murdered those who stood in the way of their hauling off whatever valuable goods they could find. There were plenty: plates of gold and silver, icons studded with jewels, silver crosses, and priests' vestments. There was so much booty that mules were driven up to the altar for loading. As a final insult to the Greek Christians, they enthroned a common whore in the Patriarchal throne to sing lewd songs and dance. Hardly any major city in Europe was without a souvenir of the crusaders' behaviour. St Mark's in Venice particularly benefitted; its celebrated bronze horses and vast collection of Byzantine plate are war booty. The Shroud seemed to have gone 'underground' during this turbulent period and Sir Steven Runciman has suggested that 'some private looter took the relic, and if we do not hear of it again till 1356, it was because it was in private hands – and perhaps rather embarrassed private hands as they had no proper title to it. Only a century and a half later could it emerge without embarrassment.'

There have been various attempts made to bridge the gap of years from 1204 to 1356, from Constantinople to Lirey. According to the historian, Dom Chamard, a shroud corresponding to De Clari's description was deposited in the hands of the Archbishop of Besançon, by Ponce de la Roche, the father of Othon de la Roche, who was one of the leaders of the Burgundian army in the fourth crusade. Dom Chamard carried this theory a step further. The Besançon Cathedral was destroyed by fire in 1349. During the conflagration the Shroud was stolen and given to Geoffrey de Charny, who placed it in the church at Lirey. To assure himself of permanent possession, Geoffrey had a painted copy of the frontal imprint made, and this he palmed off on the cathedral chapter of Besançon which they supposedly accepted without suspicion. This was examined by the authorities in 1794 and revealed to be a painted copy.[29]

Adam Otterbein's article in the *New Catholic Encyclopedia* suggested, '. . . It was not unlikely that (the Shroud) was taken to France at the time when the fall of Constantinople to the Orientals was foreseen. Further, it is known that the Latin Emperor's minister who had access to (the Shroud), returned to the West shortly before the fall of Constantinople. He was of the family of the wife of Geoffrey de Charny . . .' This notion assumes that the Latins expected Constantinople to collapse easily and also it seems incredible that the Latin Emperor Baldwin II would have allowed such a major relic to depart without a definite destination, when considering his poor financial condition, he would surely have tried to raise money on it.

The French Jesuit, Paul de Gail, feels that the cloth remained in Constantinople after the 1204 sack of the city. It is known that the relics that were kept in the Bucoleon chapel were left where they were as the property of the new Latin Emperor. Since Baldwin II presented St Louis, the French King, with a small portion of the Shroud as a gift, it is assumed that this was done under his supervision. The Emperor was still disposing of such articles as the Crown of Thorns and True Cross fragments in 1238–1241. Clearly some of the Byzantine treasures had not been lost at the time of the Crusader sack. By 1239, Baldwin II was in such desperate financial straights that he sold the lead from his roofs and even pawned his own son. Next he set about disposing of the remaining relics in the treasury. The Crown of Thorns passed to Venetian money-lenders and was purchased by St Louis from them. In 1247 the French King persuaded the Emperor to issue a Golden Bull transferring all rights of other possessions to him. Among the listed articles was the Image of Edessa.[30]

St Louis had his portion of the Shroud and probably the

Image of Edessa among his vast collection to be elegantly displayed in the Sainte Chapelle, but the Shroud itself followed another route in de Gail's analysis. The historian places great importance to the statements of Geoffrey II de Charny and his daughter that Geoffrey I had received the Shroud as a 'war prize' or 'gift of war'. Also the French knight had stated to the Lirey collegiale that he had obtained the cloth in the 'war against the infidels'. The only situation to fit these requirements historically was the Dauphin's crusade of 1343–1346, the sole war enterprise in which Geoffrey I de Charny had fought the infidels.[31] During this campaign the fleet of Hugh IV of Cyprus supported the 'league of Pope Clement VI' which took the city of Smyrna in 1343. De Gail feels that the Knights Templar, 'benevolent receivers of relics and stolen goods' had the Shroud in their possession at this time. He further suggests that it was either given or sold to them by the desperate Baldwin. When the order was disbanded, it came into the hands of the Hospitallers, who inherited the Templar possessions and affairs. So the Shroud was part of the war booty of Smyrna and Geoffrey I de Charny was 'just the type of princely knight in whose care it could be entrusted!' Geoffrey returned to France immediately after the Smyrna enterprise, and the Shroud would have to be with him. The strength of de Gail's thesis is the insistence of the de Charny family that the relic had been a gift of war; the weakness is the lack of documentation of a transfer from Constantinople to Smyrna – from Baldwin II to the Templars and the Hospitallers.

Few writers have worked harder in recent years to supply the Shroud with a complete history than the Oxford history graduate, Ian Wilson. In a sense, Wilson has carried the work of Paul Vignon and Maurus Green to a logical conclusion that the Turin Shroud is one and the same as one of the most celebrated icon images of Christ, the Holy Mandylion of the Syro-Byzantine city of Edessa.

During the 1930s the French writer, Paul Vignon, noted that many Byzantine images of Jesus reveal peculiarities which can be seen in the Shroud and appear like copies of the

Shroud's face. These peculiar markings included: long hair with two or three wisps of hair on the forehead, a three-sided 'square' between the eyebrows, a 'V' shape at the bridge of the nose, a raised right eyebrow, staring eyes, a long straight nose with enlarged left nostril, swollen cheeks, forked beard, divided moustache and a transverse mark across the throat. Many icon images seemed to repeat a number of these markings and suggested an archetype. We find this 'new image' appearing in the sixth century.[32]

Older traditions have Jesus' physical appearance as small and ugly, like Socrates. Origen seems to accept this description and Clement of Alexandria hints that Jesus' face was ugly. This view would seem to be based on a literal acceptance of Jesus' identification with Isaiah's 'suffering servant', '. . . he had no form of comeliness that we should look at him, and no beauty that we should desire him.' (Isaiah 53.2).

The earliest portrayals of Jesus in Christian art were generally of an Apollo or young shepherd type. Even these symbolic representations had to overcome the inherited Jewish scruple against the use of art for religion. The frequent choice of Jesus as the Good Shepherd was a natural one. Its appropriateness in the catacombs was obvious – the young shepherd leading his sheep 'through the valley of the shadow of death'. Christ in this form, as exquisitely seen in the third century Lateran Museum statue, was so plainly a symbol that it was not thought to be an abused form and it had its easily recognisable pagan parallel in the romantic figure of good husbandry and economy.[33] This was true also of the mid-third century *Sol Invictus* on a mosaic found under St Peter's – easily adapted to the Christian belief in the risen Lord. Three centuries or so following these representations we find the beginnings of an image of Jesus which has remained to this day the basis of our popular portrayals of what Jesus looked like. Christ the 'Pantocrator' and the image 'not made with hands' were to be among the standard representations of Jesus throughout the Byzantine world and would gradually supplant the older images in Italy as well.

Perhaps one of the oldest prototypes for this new image of

Jesus was the Edessa Mandylion. An early Syriac account of the story of its origin, *The Doctrine of Addai*, has a messenger, Ananias, sent by King Abgar of Edessa to interview the prophet Jesus. Ananias returns not only with his verbal impression of Jesus but also a portrait which he painted 'with choice colours'. The historical Abgar of this account was probably Abgar V, a contemporary of Christ, who reigned in Edessa from 4 BC to AD 50. The earliest known telling of the Abgar story by Eusebius of Caesarea in his AD 325 history makes no mention of the portrait. A version written about four centuries later by John of Damascus has Ananias unable to re-create the brilliance of Jesus' countenance with the result that Jesus held a cloth to his face causing his portrait to be miraculously printed on the material. Sir Steven Runciman in what is considered to be one of the definitive works on the Edessa Image in the *Cambridge Historical Journal* wrote:

> It is easy to show that the story of Abgar and Jesus as we now have it is untrue, that the letters contain phrases copied from the gospels and are framed according to the dictates of later theology. But that does not necessarily invalidate the tradition on which the story was based: and while we may respect the anxious incredulity that characterises modern believers, we should recognise that there is no reason why King Abgar V should not have suffered from the religious curiosity fashionable at the time, and should not have heard of the Messiah in Palestine and sent to learn more.[34]

Runciman has further suggested that during the sixth century religious strife when Monophysite Jacob Baradaeus became bishop of Edessa perhaps some orthodox cleric joined the old tradition of the portrait sent to Abgar 'an old icon, whose origin we cannot hope to trace,' and thus by 'a timely political move against the heretics . . . gave the legend new vitality by providing it with the concrete accompaniment that orthodox piety was beginning to demand'.[35]

Edessa was one of the earliest Christian centres and probably the Mandylion tradition was related in some sense to the

King's conversion and many of the city's leading citizens. When persecution of Christians arose under his non-Christian successor, the cloth disappeared but was later discovered sealed inside a niche in the city's wall. It was promptly accepted as the *acheiropoietos*, 'not made with hands', and so coveted by the Byzantine emperors. In 943, it was purchased by Constantinople for 12,000 silver coins, 200 captives and the guarantee of Edessa's immunity from attack. According to H. C. Bowen's account in *Ali Ibn-Isa*, the Christian inhabitants of Edessa were exceedingly reluctant to part with their blessed image: they tried in vain to foist a copy on the bishop sent to receive it and only yielded in the end to the threats of the Muslim commander (Edessa had fallen to conquest by this time).[36] But at length it was removed with ceremony to Constantinople, performing a series of miracles on the way. Now it was in the hands of the Emperor and was given a grand reception in a city already overloaded with a huge treasury of relics, but as Runciman states it soon fell into the background. 'There were too many rivals at Constantinople.' Where the image was to be kept would in time come to be the setting for almost every important relic of the church: the Crown of Thorns, pieces of the True Cross, a container of Holy Blood, the lance which pierced Christ's side, his seamless coat and many others. 'In such company this . . . cloth was impressive only to those who knew its history and in time few remembered that glorious past.'

Linking the Turin Shroud with the Edessa Image is difficult because the latter has always been presented in its representations as a head-only portrait of Jesus and, according to all the traditions, one which was made before his death. Wilson feels that this has been made easier by his commissioning a teacher and students of West Yorkshire's Bradford Grammar School to make the full-length English translation of the official history of the image, *De Imagine Edessena*. This was written by a member of the tenth century court of Emperor Constantine Porphyrogenitus and there the image is described as composed of 'a moist secretion without coloring or painter's art' in one of the many accounts of the article.[37] Wilson places great importance to a footnote in Roberts and Donaldson's translation of the Abgar legend where the word 'towel' (which Jesus used to wipe his face, leaving the imprint) is translated with some difficulty as 'doubled in four' *(tetradiplon)*. Wilson was intrigued by this: 'Could the sixth-century writer have been trying to convey that the cloth he saw was literally "doubled in four" – i.e., that it was a substantially larger cloth, the folds perhaps being actually countable at the edges but otherwise inaccessible?' Going the next step was obvious – folding a photograph of the Turin Shroud does reveal a strikingly 'head only' section. Wilson suggests that this final folding was stretched tautly on a board and covered with a trellis-style embellishment, 'significantly in a style common to the ornamentation on the costumes of monarchs of the Parthian period'. In the Byzantine liturgical texts, the Edessa image was so highly venerated that few ever saw it directly. What was seen were the many artists' representations in icon form such as the thirteenth century Holy Face of Laon, a Slavic copy. This century also saw the beginning of a considerable Russian interest in the 'Christ-not-made-with-hands' which became an important icon representation for all Russian churches. The earliest pictorial evidence of the Edessa image to have survived is on a possibly tenth century painted icon kept in St Catherine's monastery at Mt. Sinai. King Abgar (who is seen as Constantine Porphyrogenitus, according to most experts) is holding the image represented as a youngish head of Christ with a nimbus – little resemblance to the Shroud face there.

Wilson bridges the gap from Edessa–Constantinople to Lirey through the same group as de Gail – the Knights Templar. Some accounts of the Templars say they worshipped an unidentified bearded male head, among other things, at their secret chapter meetings. The order was suppressed in 1307, having been accused on a variety of counts including idolatry and heresy. Recently on the site of an old Templar preceptory in Templecombe, Somerset, a painted head was found bearing an uncanny likeness to the Shroud Face.

In 1314, two leading Knights Templar were brought to a small island in the Seine to be burned at the stake. One was the Grand Master, Jacques de Molay[38] the other, Geoffrey de Charnay.[39] What connection, if any, there be between this Geoffrey and the first recorded owner of the Shroud, Geoffrey de Charny, is not known. The Knights Templar were a celibate order. Wilson has speculated that there is a relationship and indeed this is the answer to the de Charny family's reticence to publicise their prized relic. The ignominy of the family connection with the damned Knights Templar was still strong in their minds.

Some who have read Wilson's thesis are not convinced by his evidence. Steven Runciman pinpointed the following problems: '. . . the Image of Edessa was always described by the Byzantines as a "mandelion", a kerchief, which is quite different from a "sindon". Besides, as we know from the lists of Byzantine relics,[40] they believed that they possessed the Holy Shroud, which is listed separately by them. I cannot think it helps the Shroud to force its identification with the Image, particularly when it means a rather oversimplification of the Abgar legend. If we are going to convince people of the reality of the relic I think we should be careful what we claim for it.'

Forcing the identification of the two creates other difficulties:

1. Even the later usages of the terms *mandylion* and *sindon* in Byzantine liturgical practices stood for very different articles. The *mandylion* came to mean the decorative veil at the top of an icon; the epitaphios *sindon* (this article is discussed in a chapter note) was a large cloth brought in procession at the Great Entry of the Eucharist and was frequently carried on the heads of the officiating clergy.

2. Aside from referring to both Shroud and Mandylion as separate treasures Robert de Clari reported to have seen two copies of the Image of Edessa on tiles. He makes no mention of any relationship between the two, disguised or otherwise.

3. It seems odd that the disciples would let their Lord's

shroud go in a disguised form to a city relatively unknown to them.

4. The trellis background Wilson imagines as concealing the true nature of the Shroud was widely used in the Orthodox world by icon painters and embroiderers. It is to be found on numerous icons, not just those of Christ in the *acheiropoietos* form.

5. The Mandylion-style icons Wilson cites for reference to his circular shaped, trellis covered concealment (such as the *Spas Nereditsa*) were more probably designed from precise allegorical measurements rather than being duplications of a disguised Shroud face.[41]

6. Historians of the history of the Image of Edessa, De Riant, von Dobschutz and Runciman see the Mandylion's end with the destruction of the Sainte Chapelle during the French Revolution. There is an alternative destruction given by Andre Grabar in an early edition of his writing on the Holy Face of Laon: 'In 1204, when Constantinople was taken by the Latin Crusaders, (the Mandylion), at the distribution of the booty, was given away to the Venetian Doge Dandolo, who sent it away by sea to Venice. The ship sank in the sea of Marmara with all on it.'[42]

The icon *acheiropoietos* occupied and still does in Orthodoxy a central place among the images of Christ. The idea 'not made with hands' is deeply rooted in Scripture (as in Mark 14.58) and incarnational theology and gave great importance to the making of icons. By the fourth century there was the feeling that no mortal hand could have painted the divine image and by the start of the fifth century the tradition had acquired a legendary form and impetus in the stories of Abgar. These stories expressed in their naive manner a dogmatic truth: Christian iconography had its foundation in God made flesh. The consequence of this was logical for the artists: the sacred art of icons was not an arbitrary creation of the artists anymore than theologians' words. Both were *acheiropoietos*. Perhaps the Turin Shroud was the inspiration for the Edessa icon – kept as Paul Vignon suspected in some monastery easily accessible to the theologians and artists of Edessa, but surely no justice is done in forcing an identification of the Shroud with the Mandylion.

Wilson and de Gail have gone a long way in an attempt to cover the more difficult historical gaps but there will always be some insurmountable obstacles facing the search for the Shroud's early history. We first have to face the fact that to the Jews and early Christians anything having to do with a corpse was impure – there would have been a considerable embarrassment in retaining such an article publicly. The Eastern reticence to portraying Jesus' crucified body in any realistic fashion has an obvious bearing on the Shroud's retention. Even as late as the fifteenth century, the depiction of the dead Christ on those curious liturgical shrouds, the *epitaphioi*,[43] was restrained and removed from his actual physical passion. As we have seen, it was a long time in the West as well until we had crucifixion scenes such as those we know so well today. Gregory of Tours relates that as late as the sixth century in France reaction was so strong against a painted image of the dead Jesus on a cross that one bishop covered the crucifix with a veil.

The problems over retaining the Shroud continue when we face the other possible owners: an unnamed Crusader looter, the Templars, the Hospitallers and the de Charny family. How was it that Geoffrey de Charny, an unimportant figure in the political spectrum should possess the burial cloth of Jesus after its being a part of the splendid Byzantine court? Why should it be his war booty or a gift for services rendered? Why should the Templars entrust it to him considering the possibilities open to them? Perhaps Runciman is right in suggesting that the Shroud might have come out of Constantinople in the hands of a private looter as many treasures and relics did. Writing in *The Great Betrayal*, Ernle Bradford states that '. . . although $\frac{3}{8}$ of the relics in the city were officially allotted to the clergy, it was not only the Roman Catholic priests who scavenged through the churches, convents and monasteries. The knights, men-at-arms and common soldiers were equally superstitious and undoubtedly many of them felt that only by obtaining possession of some holy relic might their crime of having attacked the city be assuaged.'[44]

Perhaps this forever unidentifiable looter gave the Shroud to Geoffrey I de Charny and his progeny were reticent to say anything more about their having it than that it was 'war booty' or a 'gift'. There are no documents, as we have seen, to indicate that it was officially presented to de Charny, and there is not even the evidence to suggest that he built the church in Lirey for the purpose of containing the relic. He downplayed his possession of it – maybe because he was embarrassed by the circumstances through which he came to possess it. This might also explain Bishop d'Arcis' refusal to accept it as genuine. There were no papers of transfer and the relic had been kept in the court of the Byzantines. How dare a fairly ordinary knight claim it was a family treasure?

At every turn we are up against a wall of reticence. Perhaps this was the most important reason for the Shroud's survival and at the same time the reason we will probably never have a satisfactory early history for the cloth. But is a documented historical pedigree all that important? When a questionable work of art is examined, it is rare that historians can fully authenticate it. More likely it goes to the laboratory where the canvas and pigments are examined and the method of application is scrutinised. After the specialists have done all they possibly can and after the object is considered on its own merits, then and only then do the art historian and critic give valuable advice as to where it might have come from and to what period it belongs. The history of an art object can be faked much more easily than the work itself. The facts for its history may be lacking or confused but none of this really affects the matter of its final authentication. We must face the possibility that the Turin Shroud may never have a total historical pedigree. We must also face the basic fact that the relic purports to be the only remains we have of Jesus – the Son of God to millions of people. This so colours the situation as to make objective study, scientifically and historically, an extremely delicate matter.

When Yves Delage wrote of the arraignment he faced after his presentation of the Shroud's authenticity to the French Academy in 1902, he spoke some wise words still very applicable to the matter:

> If they (my hypotheses) have not received from certain people the welcome they deserved, the sole reason is that there has been unfairly grafted on to this scientific question a religious issue which excites men's minds and misleads right reason. If not Christ but Sargon or Achilles or one of the Pharaohs had been involved, no one would have any objection. I consider Christ as an historical person, and I see no reason why people should be scandalised if there exists a material trace of his existence.

CHAPTER 4

WHAT HAS SCIENCE SAID ABOUT THE SHROUD IN THE PAST?

'An Alleged Miracle . . . after eighteen centuries, an authentic likeness of Jesus Christ has been obtained,' announced the *Osservatore Romano*, the official organ of the Vatican.

'It seems that King Umberto is the possessor of a winding-sheet which is reported to have been used by Joseph of Arimathea for wrapping the body of Jesus when he was taken from the cross, and that on the sheet are a number of almost imperceptible blood-stains, which have been said to faintly outline the contour of the body . . . the details of which are said to come out so beautifully that they look more like portraits from the body than any shroud or picture . . .' (*The Photogram*, 1898).

A canon of Turin Cathedral gave this description to a correspondent of the *Daily Telegraph*: 'The Redeemer, who miraculously left the imprint of his sufferings, and the lines of his body, on the Shroud that enveloped him in the tomb, has miraculously reappeared on a photographic plate, with a perfection of detail that causes stupefaction. The noble figure has come forth anatomically elegant, perfect and divinely beautiful. The countenance is still marked with ineffable suffering. All the details are there . . . In a word, the photograph of the sacred Shroud has given forth His portrait.'

'The rumour of the marvellous event spread like wildfire in Turin. His Grace the Archbishop, Duchess Isabella, Princess Clara, illustrious prelates, artists, business men hastened to the studio of Signor Pia to investigate the truth of the rumour. They were one and all convinced. A noted archaeologist and artist, who had previously expressed doubts as to the authenticity of the Shroud, was now forced to exclaim: "Either this is the true shroud, or it is a god who painted it.' (*The Photogram*, 1898).

This was one manner in which the news of the photographing of the Turin Shroud was presented in the press in 1898, the year which marked the beginning of the scientific study of the relic.[45] Seconda Pia, the first photographer of the Shroud, came from a family of ancient Piedmontese descent and noteworthy public service. He studied law and was elected mayor of Asti. Pia's interest in the history and art of Piedmont led him to be a member of the organising body for the Exhibition of Sacred Art which would coincide with the exposition of the Shroud in 1898 to honour the recent marriage of King Victor Emmanuel III and also the anniversary of the *Statuto*, the constitution of the new Italian kingdom. It was only natural for Turin, the centre city for the unification of Italy, to celebrate in a grand manner. Pia, who had a passion for the new art of photography, suggested to the president of the executive committee of the exhibition, Baron Antonio Manno, that advantage should be taken of the public showing of the Shroud to have it photographed. Picture copies of the precious relic could be made available to the pious and knowledge of its existence would then be easily disseminated around the world. There is no doubt that this was Pia's only motive in making the suggestion. Photography, however, was not an accepted art and there was fear that the cold reproducing machine might damage the relic. There was also the concern that commercial exploitation might be made with the photographs of the cloth. A change in this attitude of the royal family and the curia occurred with a letter by Pia to Baron Manno 'renouncing any kind of copyrights and bearing all expenses incurred by me in connection with this work' and assuring the Baron he would have 'no part in any kind of speculation which my work might suggest to others'. Baron Manno, a member of the Heraldic Council was the right man for the diplomatic overture at Court.

The next hurdles were to be even more difficult. The last exposition of the Shroud had been in 1868 when Pia was a small boy and observations of those who had seen it then were vague and unhelpful. But even more formidable was the problem of lighting. It was impossible to photograph the cloth in daylight because there was to be no open air showing. Pia was left with the chancy situation of having to find adequate artificial light, a practice not offering an abundance of experience in 1898. The placing of the stretched cloth in a frame above the altar required the building of a scaffolding for a good working position and there would be precious little time available for him to photograph during the brief interval between the initial ceremony and the showing to the public. Strikes forced a postponement of the exposition from 11 May to 25 May, and Pia's first attempt ended in utter frustration. In trying to correct the lighting in the Cathedral, he put two frosted glasses in front of the lights to get a more even and diffused effect but the heat produced by the lamps broke the glasses. He would have to begin again the next day. Pia started work again at 9.30 p.m. on 28 May, and this time there was a protective glass placed over the relic at the insistence of Princess Clotilde who had a deep devotion to the cloth and was fearful that it was being contaminated by the smoke from the incense and candles. Added to this was the considerable variability in the electric current and at the moment of placing the camera on the scaffolding it was discovered that almost all the necessary bolts for the structure had disappeared. The head of the security service at the Cathedral, Lieutenant Felice Fino, came to the rescue. He and his men managed as well as possible to secure the scaffolding. Fino was also an ardent devotee of the art of photography and he with another enthusiast, Father Sanna Solaro, took their own photographs which were to prove invaluable in supporting Pia's findings. The darkroom was nearby, and it was to be the scene of a considerable surprise. Pia saw slowly appearing on the negative plate an image which could not be imagined when looking at the faint impression on the cloth. The photographer was astonished to see that his negative was a far more informative and life-like image than the original on the cloth. The 'original' face was restored on the negative. The Shroud impression was apparently itself a 'negative' image from which a 'positive' could be obtained by simply making a photographic negative. No one had seen the depth and clarity of the relic's images until this moment when the light values were reversed by the camera. All the difficulties Pia had had to face were worth that discovery. Pia's surprise was such that he nearly dropped the large and heavy plate. Unknowingly he had started the scientific exploration of the Shroud with the large 'reproducing box'.

Some of the reaction to the photographs was contradictory. There was the charge that they were created by overexposure. This was easily discounted by comparing the similar results of Father Solaro and Lieutenant Fino as well as the fact that the two angels on the sides of the relic's frame did not appear in 'positive' like the Shroud. Some reporters insisted that the results were an 'image appearing by chance or optical illusion'. These criticisms were nothing compared to the long-lasting attack which was to come from the formidable pen of the illustrious French scholar, Canon Cyr Ulysse Chevalier, described by one commentator as 'the most learned man in France and perhaps in the entire world'. While still in seminary, he was elected to the National Historical Society of France and at thirty-six he became a knight of the Legion of Honour. Not many months after Pia's darkroom discovery, Chevalier studied the results and began to pursue the history of this unusual relic. As we saw in the last chapter, his research led him to conclude that the cloth was a forgery. So influential was his view of the situation that it remained the semi-official position in the old *Catholic Encyclopedia* article on the Shroud by the English Jesuit, Herbert Thurston. One of his conclusions was 'this shroud like the others was probably painted . . . in a yellowish tint upon unbleached linen, the marks of wounds being added in brilliant red'. Chevalier's strongest argument had been his insistence that the Congregation of Indulgences and Relics had given an unofficial verdict against the authenticity of the Turin Shroud. This case was not fully closed until Luigi Fossati reported in the March 1960 issue of *Sindon* having received the following reply from the Congregation on 30 November 1959: 'No document regarding the Holy Shroud of Turin of the sort described by Chevalier exists in the files of the Sacred Congregation of Indulgences and Relics, at present in the secret archives of the Vatican.'[46]

One person who squarely faced the forgery theory of Chevalier was the Sorbonne professor, Yves Delage. In 1900 he showed Pia's photographs to a younger scientist, Paul Joseph Vignon. Their relationship would prove to be a great step in an eventual academic appreciation of the Turin cloth. Encouraged by Delage, Vignon began to tackle the forgery notion. There would have to be some telltale mistakes on the image, considering the multitude of detail made apparent by the photographs. Vignon visited Pia in Turin and returned to Paris with a clear understanding of the photographer's work and copies of his photographs plus those of Father Solaro and Lieutenant Fino. With Delage's support, Vignon spent months studying the possible forming process of the impressions on the cloth. His experiments ranged from covering himself with red chalk and then having albumen-coated linen draped over his body (the resulting impressions were greatly distorted) to a re-creation of the anointing myrrh and aloes of the Gospels. The latter led to his vaporograph theory. The body of Jesus, because of the tortures he suffered, was covered in a feverish perspiration, rich in urea, which fermented into ammonium carbonate in the damp atmosphere of the tomb. This released ammonia acted on the highly sensitive aloes sprinkled on the burial cloth, producing a stain not unlike the Shroud's in colour, the vapour acting in inverse ratio to the distance between the outlines of the body and the surface of the linen. The material was impressed by vaporography. This was how the oldest photograph in the world was created according to Vignon.

One discovery which reinforced Vignon's idea concerning the image formation was made by Dr Jean Volckringer, the chief apothecary of St Joseph's Hospital in Paris. In his researches into the formations of colours, Volckringer had noticed that with a group of pressed herbs sometimes a nearly identical image of a leaf had been formed several pages away from its original mounting. He described these images as:

> 'like a light design in sepia, perfect in continuity: examination under a magnifying glass revealed no fine lines, but a collection of stains without clearly defined boundaries. One could distinguish on the impression, which is sepia in colour, the veins of the leaves, in their smallest ramifications, and where the stalk had been cut . . . the folds and the reciprocal positions of the various parts of the plant, thanks to the comparison of the upper and lower impressions . . . The whole plant is faithfully reproduced in the two images.'

When they were photographed the result was similar to Pia's pictures of the Shroud: the 'negative' image gave the far clearer picture. This with the similar sepia colour of the original excited Barbet. With these herbals one was dealing with living tissue, albeit vegetable, and it was known that plants contain urea, uric acid, allantoine and allantoic acid. The images seemed to resist all reagents except ammonia which weakened the colour, and none of the images were to be found with recently pressed herbals – it had taken a century for the best examples to be formed. Later Dr Pierre Barbet wrote that Vignon had some important confirmation for his theory of how the Shroud images came into being – and it was a natural phenomenon: '. . . nature having spontaneously furnished us with a similar example'.

In 1902, Yves Delage, who was well known to his academic associates as an agnostic, presented a paper entitled 'The Image of Christ Visible on the Holy Shroud of Turin' to the Academy of Sciences. He painstakingly elaborated Vignon's studies and concluded that these experiments had demonstrated that the Shroud was not a forgery. The reaction was fierce in some academic circles in Paris. Delage and Vignon were ridiculed in an almost hysterical fashion by fellow scientists. Chevalier's judgment on the relic would last a long time in most academic ranks but due to the Frenchmen's efforts, a new science, sindonology, was born.

Thirty-three years after Pia's photographing, on the occasion of the marriage of Crown Prince Umberto to the Belgian princess, Maria José, the Shroud was again exhibited from 3 May to 24 May 1931. New photographs were desired and those made by the Turin photographer, Giuseppe Enrie, were a brilliant and irrefutable confirmation of the reliability of the procedure used by Pia. The latter, now seventy-six years old, was present for the photographing and was able to see an even clearer Shroud face in the tray of chemicals. The 1931 results displayed a much more complete reproduction of the shape of the body with the improved photographic techniques. The set included four entire Shroud reproductions, the complete dorsal imprint, enlargements of wound marks and sevenfold magnification of the cloth's weave. The latter would make possible helpful comparison of the linen of the Shroud with other ancient linens. Both exposure and processing took place in the presence of scientists of the French Academy which would have pleased Yves Delage. In Enrie's own analysis of his work, he saw no traces of colouring on the image or any marks made by a paint brush or any other forgering artifice. The light and shade had no contours and was without lines or stippling. On the contrary, it was in 'scarcely perceptible gradations which remind one of a photographic process'.

A friend of Dr Pierre Barbet, the head surgeon of St Joseph's Hospital in Paris, brought copies of Enrie's photographs to the doctor for anatomical examination in 1932. The results of his studies were presented in excruciating detail in *The Passion of our Lord Jesus Christ* where he stated that his 'first aim was to verify the anatomical accuracy of the marks on the Shroud'. Experiments with cadavers showed that a body suspended with nails through the palms will tear loose but, as we have seen, Barbet discovered a narrow passage through the wrists (the carpal area) that could support the weight of the body. He had also noticed the absence of thumb prints on Enrie's photographs and further experiments revealed that when a nail was driven through that particular joint in the wrist, the thumbs dropped inward upon the palm. Barbet stressed the effects of the soldiers' scourging. He found 'haematomas beneath the bleeding surfaces of the face', and excoriations could be seen especially on the right side; also the nose was 'deformed by a fracture of the posterior of the cartilage'. His analyses displayed more than fifty strokes of the Roman *flagrum* on the body. The spear-thrust was a *coup de grace* required by law in this type of execution but Jesus had already expired as the result of a tetanic contraction of the muscles that quickly reached the respiratory system. Jesus died from asphyxia in Barbet's examination. When he was able to observe the blood marks on the cloth at the 1933 outdoor exhibition,[47] he knew what he was seeing: '. . . a surgeon could understand, with no possibility of doubt, that it was blood which had sunk into the linen, and this was the Blood of Christ'.

Barbet's monumental efforts remained unchallenged by Shroud enthusiast's for a long time. One person who has attempted to look more objectively at his work is Dr Anthony Sava of New York. He has pointed to Barbet's personal piety clouding the 'boundary between subjectivity and scientific appraisal'. Dr Sava visited Barbet in 1951 and the French surgeon felt that Sava should not publish his own findings because 'they were absolutely wrong' and would confuse the public. Since Barbet was no longer young, he felt he was 'unable to become involved in any revival of controversy'. Sava has reminded us that '(Barbet) was forced to work within the limits of the medical knowledge of his day and what handicapped him even more (than his subjectivity) is the fact that by the time cadavers were available for his studies, the tissues already had lost the resiliency which is present only for a limited time after death'. Sava's disagreements with Barbet are not really very severe; he readily admits the importance of the Frenchman's achievements as does any medical analyser of the Shroud. As we saw in Chapter Three, the variances are largely over two points; the nailing through the wrist area should be located at the space between the radius and the ulna and the 'blood and water' of John's gospel was created by the scourging of Jesus, producing a bloody accumulation within the chest.

Writing in 1958, pathologist Robert Bucklin felt that:

> It would appear that perhaps the combination of the theories of Barbet and Sava might explain the situation. An accumulation of fluid in the pleural space without haemorrhage is a logical conclusion as the result of congestive heart failure related to the position of the victim on the cross. It is quite possible that there was a considerable amount of fluid so accumulated, enough so that when the lance pierced the side that fluid would be clearly seen. I feel that an actual puncture of the heart must be accepted as factual . . .[48]

Sindonology as an organised study saw total fruition in the first Congress on Shroud Studies held in 1939 in Turin. About twenty reports were presented ranging from Dr Maser's 'The Verdict of Forensic Medicine on the Imprints of the Shroud' to Roman Professor Cecchelli's 'The Dependence of Early Byzantine Iconography on the Face of the Shroud'. Never had any relic of the Roman Catholic Church received such serious attention. Popular interest in the Shroud at this time was prompted largely by two English-speaking individuals, Father Peter Rinaldi, until recently pastor of the Catholic church in Port Chester, New York and British World War II hero, Group Captain Leonard Cheshire. When the authorities in Turin were preparing for the 1933 Exposition they needed an interpreter who could speak French and English as well as Italian. They chose a young Silesian seminarian who had been born in Turin and studied in America, Peter Rinaldi. When he returned to the States after the exposition he wrote extensively about the Shroud for the general public and his *It Is The Lord* sold hundreds of thousands of copies. Rinaldi became the vehicle through whom many influential people came to know about the Turin relic and he was one of the individuals responsible for establishing the American Holy Shroud Guild which would in time come to have an important voice in seeking proper scientific investigation of the cloth. Despite constant rebuffs from the Turin ecclesiastical authorities Rinaldi diplomatically pressured for research throughout the period from the first sindonological congress down to the present time. He left his thirty year long ministry in Port Chester in 1977 to devote his full energies to Shroud research in Turin. A vivid monument was left behind at the church he served so well – a magnificent marbled chapel housing a full-size replica of the Shroud and mementoes concerning its past.

Leonard Cheshire's first experience with the Shroud was seeing a copy of it in his sanatorium room in the 1950s when he was recovering from tuberculosis. As he later said, 'And there for a full month, I did little but lie and look at that Holy Face. Here was a new experience. For in front of me was no face such as artists depict, even the best of them, but one that stood in a class all of its own, one that bore the unmistakable stamp of authenticity . . . As I gazed at it I felt compelled to enquire into its origin, and as I enquired I felt impelled not so much to go on looking (though that I certainly did), as to get up and act.' And indeed that is just what Cheshire did in time, with the same admirable energy he had put into his RAF 'dambusting' flying. Upon his discharge from the hospital, he wrote pamphlets on the Shroud, aimed as were Rinaldi's at a wide audience of readers. Then came the 'Shroud Bus', a mobile Shroud museum which the captain took all over England, lecturing on the cloth and handing out his writings. The response was tremendous and the newspapers made much of the Victoria Cross-decorated war hero enchanted by a relic. On 11 May 1955 Leonard Cheshire received a letter from Mrs Veronica Woolam of Gloucester. She knew of his interest in the Shroud and asked if her daughter, Josephine, 'could be blessed with the relic of the Holy Shroud'. Josie was a ten-year-old with osteo-myelitis in the hip and the leg. She also suffered from a lung condition and doctors offered no hope of her getting better. Josie was convinced that she would be cured if she were allowed to touch the cloth of Jesus. Although sceptical that a miracle could be accomplished, Cheshire with his usual indomitable spirit decided to try to do what he could. He was unable to journey by air because of his former tuberculosis and so they would have to undertake the trip by a long train ride which would first take them to Portugal to get the permission of ex-King Umberto to have the Shroud reliquary opened. When they arrived in Turin, word of their 'mission' had preceded them. At first there was confusion as to the best procedure. In time the Archbishop of Turin gave his permission to have the reliquary opened and the silver casket was placed on Josie's lap. It was apparent that it was the Shroud that she wished to touch and Josie boldly asked if the casket could be opened. The seals were broken and she was allowed to put her hand as far as she could inside the silk covering. All present waited for something to happen. While nothing extraordinary occurred at that time, Josie Woolam was to recover from her childhood disabilities to lead a normal life in later years, and she returned with Cheshire to view the Shroud at the 1978 exposition. This experience plus his tireless interest in the Turin cloth would make Cheshire's name synonymous with interest in the Shroud in Britain.

Two other Englishmen with quite varying approaches to the subject from that of Cheshire but who also presented a certain impetus to the research of the 1960s were Geoffrey Ashe and Leo Vala. To the journalist Ashe goes the credit for first suggesting in an article in *Sindon* that the images on the cloth were created by 'scorching'. Ashe could not accept Vignon's vaporographic theory nor any of the other theories of image creation which had been put forth. As he saw the situation: 'A great obstacle has been the impossibility of deciding what sort of picture the Shroud is, irrespective of any conjectures as to the process of its formation. Nothing quite like it has ever been produced. In particular the inverted or negative relief is thus far unparalleled.' In a very simple experiment, Ashe produced a scorch image on linen using a heated brass ornament representing a horse in relief. The result was flatter in relief than a human figure but the resemblance to the type of image we have with the Shroud is unmistakable and when Ashe made a photographic negative of his scorch picture, he got a positive image with considerable clarity. The human body, dead or alive, could not produce heat radiation strong enough to create such images but as Ashe has written:

> The Christian Creed has always affirmed that Our Lord underwent an unparalleled transformation in the tomb. His case is exceptional and perhaps here is the key. It is at least intelligible (and has indeed been suggested several times) that the physical change of the body at the Resurrection may have released a brief and violent burst of some other radiation than heat, perhaps scientifically identifiable, perhaps not, which scorched the cloth. In this case the Shroud image is a quasi-photograph of Christ returning to life, produced by a kind of radiance or 'incandescence' partially analogous to heat in its effects. Hints at some such property are supplied by narratives of the Transfiguration and the blinding of Saul. Also, the fact that the bloodstains on the Shroud are positive is now readily accounted for. The blood was matter which ceased to be part of the body, underwent no change at the Resurrection, and therefore did not scorch, but marked the cloth differently.[49]

The popular American author, John Hersey, wrote a series of penetrating observations of the effects of the atomic bombing of Hiroshima following World War II. In one of the accounts he mentioned that scientists had noticed that '. . . the flash of the bomb discoloured concrete to a light reddish tint . . . and had scorched other types of building material, and that consequently had, in some places, left prints of the shadows that had been cast by its light'.[50] A permanent shadow was thrown across the roof of the Chamber of Commerce building and, most interestingly, a few vague human silhouettes were found.

Ashe's 'radiation theory' would come to be discussed by other writers and a number of scientists later when more was discovered about the penetration of image on the Turin cloth. The one-time fashion photographer and agnostic, Leo Vala of London, first became interested in the Shroud because he suspected that it was created by some sort of photographic process. After some investigation he would be able to declare, 'I can prove conclusively that claims calling the Shroud a fake are completely untrue. Even with today's highly advanced photographic resources nobody alive could produce the image – a photographic negative – embodied in the Shroud'.[51] Vala attracted considerable attention in the 1960s by producing a three dimensional 'sculpture' from the Mona Lisa. It was only natural that he would become interested in turning the flat surface of the 'world's oldest photograph' into a profile. Vala explained his method in the following manner to the *British Journal of Photography*:

> . . . a short period of blindness made me think more about vision than one normally does . . . Photographers look at a picture and use all their skills to photograph solid objects and bring them down to a two-dimensional picture . . . If we had a vehicle for it we could take a flat object and commit it back into solid. This is the basis of my process, which is very simple. It is a question of interpreting one's vision about the two-dimensional image and putting it in terms of depth. With a photographic image this is easily understandable. If I photograph a human head from here, the nose is nearer and the ears further away and on the final picture the nose will be larger and the ears smaller. Now if a transparency is made and projected back on a lump of clay this can be automatically corrected, since for example, the projector being further away from the ears on the bust will automatically bring these back to proper size. In this way, and by finding the depth information recorded in shadows and highlights, it is possible to obtain a solid representation.

Using two projectors with transparencies of Enrie's Shroud face in each, he projected them on to his sculptured 'lump of clay' which he could further mould into correction according to the three-dimensional image cast upon it. The result was striking: the broken nose cartilage, the swellings and abrasions – they were all there, as well as an impressive overall image of majesty.

While Vala was displaying his creation in his London studio, nearly two thousand miles away north of the Damascus Gate of the old city of Jerusalem, Israeli workmen were digging the foundation of a new housing estate. Work was stopped when they discovered three burial caves containing fifteen ossuaries, and archaeologists from the Israeli Department of Antiquities and Museums were summoned. They distinguished some thirty-five individual remains; the most interesting was to be found in ossuary I/4. Alongside the bones of a three to four year old child were discovered 'the only extant remains from antiquity known to be evidence of a crucifixion'.[52] The name *Jehohanan* and the possible identification of his occupation as 'potter' in Aramaic were deciphered from the inscription outside his burial place. Jehohanan was described in the offical report in this manner: a 24–28 year old male with a remarkably mild featured and pleasant face, and a very proportionate body, 'agreeable to sight, particularly in motion and because of the gracious, almost feminine allure; it reminds us of the Hellenistic ideal *ephebe*'. He had never engaged in heavy corporeal labour and was never seriously injured – until crucifixion itself, which was speculated as having occurred possibly in A.D. 7 when the Jews rose up in protest over a Roman census. Nicu Haas of the Department of Anatomy of the Hebrew University admitted, 'An initial anthropological approach to the first material evidence of a crucifixion does not exclude a certain emotional concern.' Apparently nails used in crucifixion were thought to be able to cure epilepsy by the Romans and others. This certainly would help explain why we have so few surviving examples.

Both the heel bones of Jehohanan were transfixed by a

large iron nail which had struck a tough knot in the olive wood, so that it could not be easily detached by the executioners. Hence the feet were chopped off above the ankle with the nail still in them, were buried with the rest of the remains. The shins were intentionally broken and although the bones of the left arm were poorly preserved, it was evident to Dr Haas that a scratch on the right radius indicated that the victim had been crucified through the forearm region. The application of the Jehohanan studies to the Shroud was soon seen: how could a forger know that the palms were not the area nailed to the cross? Almost all portrayals in art showed the palm.

More than a decade before the Jehohanan discovery, graves excavated by Père de Vaux at Khirbet Qumran attracted the attention of British Shroud enthusiast, Vera Barclay, because of the position of some of the buried skeletons which were exactly like the Turin Shroud figure. Photographs displayed the flatly stretched out, upward face, folded hands with resulting protruding elbows. As Miss Barclay put it: 'We now have definite confirmation that at the time of Christ some Jews did bury their dead in the actual position of the image on the Shroud. The projecting elbows would not have been convenient for the close winding of the Egyptian way.'[53]

Pia's accidental discovery of the negative–positive character of the Shroud in 1898 marked the beginning of serious scientific study of the cloth. Vignon, Delage, Barbet, Enrie and others each contributed unique personal observations of the Shroud's mysteries. Rinaldi and Cheshire plus a number of other devotees brought the relic to the attention of the general public. By the end of the 1960s it looked as if much had been said about the nature of the Turin cloth. No one then could have suspected how greatly accelerated the pace of serious study would become.

CHAPTER 5

DID JESUS DIE ON THE CROSS

The Jewish historian, Flavius Josephus, writing not long after the death of Jesus, called crucifixion 'the most pitiable of all forms of death' and related in his autobiography how one captive recovered from this execution:

> And when I was sent . . . to a certain village called Thecoa, in order to know where it were a place fit for a camp, as I came back, I saw many captives crucified; and remembered three of them as my former acquaintances. I was very sorry at this in my mind, and went to Titus (the general commander), and told of them; so he immediately commanded them to be taken down, and to have the greatest care taken of them, in order to their recovery; yet two of them died under the physician's hands, while the one recovered.

This one episode of recovery became 'evidence' for writers who maintained that Jesus survived the cross. The short time that Jesus hung on the cross, together with the sometimes reported tardiness of death by crucifixion, and the uncertain nature and effects of the wound from the spear, appeared to render the reality of the death doubtful in these writers' eyes. Added to this would be the general difficulty of distinguishing deep swoons from real death, and the low state of medical science in the age of Jesus.

Hugh Schonfield's fascinating and dramatic bestseller published in the 1960s, *The Passover Plot*, was the first book to popularise a view that Schliermacher and Venturini had put forward in the eighteenth century; that Jesus swooned and recovered in the cool tomb. Several writers in our own day maintain that remains of conscious life and careful medical attention, although not even hinted at in the Evangelists, were present in the case of Christ. According to Schonfield's book: 'Jesus had been convinced that his crucifixion would not be the end. Provided that he faithfully discharged the duties incumbent upon him as the Messiah . . . he was assured that God would exalt him . . . The glorification would be initiated by his resurrection . . .' On the first page, the 'plot' to make this possible is summarised:

> It is the moment before sundown in Jerusalem. On the hill of Golgotha three bodies are suspended on crosses. Two – the thieves – are dead. The third appears so. This is the drugged body of Jesus of Nazareth, the man who planned his own crucifixion, who contrived to be given a soporific potion to put him into a deathlike trance. Now Joseph of Arimathea, bearing clean linen and spices, approaches and recovers the still form of Jesus. All seems to be proceeding to plan . . .

Carl Friedrich Bahrdt writing in the 1780s had put it in a similar manner. Jesus had exposed himself to crucifixion and pretended the end had come with an early bowing of the head, knowing that he would be removed speedily from the cross and medically cared for as pre-arranged by his colleagues. The 'resurrection' appearance would follow, inspiring his forlorn disciples. Writers who did not wish to involve Jesus in such a contrived plotting suggested that he had lost consciousness on the cross and sunk into a comatose state. Body temperatures would have been lowered, the skin would have turned ashen, the legs would be swollen and breathing hardly discernible. By the definition of death in that day, it would be assumed that Jesus was dead. His 'resurrection' would be effected by a three day recovery in the tomb. Some went so far as to suggest that it was Jesus who rolled away the stone at the entrance to the tomb and, being naked, found the gardener's clothes with which to cover himself – hence Mary

Magdalene's confusion that he was the gardener when he appeared to her.

David Friedrich Strauss, the brilliant rationalist writer of *A New Life Of Jesus* in 1865, laboriously analysed all the theories of 'the Resurrection of Jesus Not a Natural Revival' and put forward a strong comment on all these speculations:

> It is impossible that a being who had stolen half-dead out of the sepulchre, weak and ill, wanting medical treatment, who required bandaging, strengthening and indulgence, and who still, at last, yielded to his sufferings, could have given to the disciples the impression that he was a Conqueror over death and the grave, the Prince of Life, an impression which lay at the bottom of their future ministry. Such a resuscitation could only have weakened the impression which he had made upon them in life and in death, at the most could only have given it an elegiac voice, but could by no possibility have changed their sorrow into enthusiasm, have elevated their reverence into worship.[54]

A theft of the body of Jesus, a plot to have him removed from the cross before he died, a resuscitation of Jesus in the coolness of the tomb – all these notions have to face the fact that his little band of followers were utterly transformed from their deep depression and utter hopelessness at his death to a strong faith and enthusiasm at Easter and Pentecost.

One group which has added the 'Shroud' evidence to a long-standing belief that Jesus did not die on the cross has been the Ahmadiyya sect of Muslims, founded in Pakistan in the latter part of the nineteenth century by Hazrat Mirza Ghulam Ahmad who had announced that God had appointed him the Messiah. 'For the first time and under Divine inspiration'[55] he proclaimed in 1890 that Jesus did not die on the cross. Like all Muslims the group accepts Jesus as a true prophet of God 'born without the agency of an earthly father, but he was not the Son of God'. The Ahmadiyya group is not accepted in Pakistan as an orthodox segment of Islam and out of the two million Muslims in Britain, only 11,000 are of this sect. Despite this they have launched an expensive campaign to win new members, feeling that Britain is a ripe field for conversion. The campaign culminated in an international symposium on 'The Deliverance of Jesus from the Cross'. Scriptural (Bible and Koran), and historical evidence was presented to show that 'Jesus escaped the accursed death on the cross'. The 'scientific evidence' presented was the Turin Shroud! Vague assertions were made that a 'large body of Christian scientists' thought that the image on the linen was that of a still living person. To them the Shroud clearly shows a man 'in the prime of his life (33 years) (who) enjoyed excellent health . . . (one who) could not be expected to have died within so short a time'.

A small group from their London Mosque headed by Iman B. A. Rafiq attended a symposium on the Shroud in September 1977. (See Chapter Seven). In the open discussion period, Iman Rafiq related how they believe that Jesus not only survived but following his recovery, he set out from Palestine in search of the 'Lost Tribes of Israel'. According to the teaching of Hazrat Ahmad, Jesus went into a swoon because of his wounds and was taken down alive from the cross and nursed by his disciples who used a special ointment (the myrhh and aloes of Nicodemus). Hazrat Ahmad seemed to think this preparation was part of a pre-arranged plot, rather than, as we have seen, a normal procedure in Jewish burial customs. Pilate's scheme to save Jesus is more detailed and contrived than Schonfield's Passover plot or Bahrdt's 1780 theory. The reason for this determination to remove Jesus from the 'accursed death' is the firm Muslim conviction that no true messenger of God would have been allowed to be so treated. The implications of the Muslim attitude for Jews and Christians are self-evident in the Ahmadiyya writings:

'The Jews believe that Jesus died on the cross because he was a false prophet . . . Modern Christianity rests on the belief that he did not die on the cross. But if it is proved that he did not die on the cross nor rise from the dead, then the whole edifice of Christianity tumbles to the ground.'

A convincing scheme would be necessary and Hazrat Ahmad supplied one: Pilate was thoroughly certain of the innocence of Jesus and goaded by his dream-troubled wife and so had a pre-planned plot to save Jesus' life:

> As a responsible official of the Roman Empire he could not openly come to the forefront, but he was the master-mind before the whole scheme and the chief actor in the drama. Other characters of the show were Joseph of Arimathea, an honourable councillor and the disciple of Jesus Christ. He had already had a sepulchre hewn out in a rock garden nearby. Another actor in the drama was a learned Jew named Nicodemus who was in the know of the whole matter . . . It was very clever of Pilate to choose Friday afternoon as the time for Jesus' crucifixion so that he could not remain on the cross after sunset, the following day being the Sabbath . . . He selected Joseph and Nicodemus as the most trusted friends to execute the prearranged scheme. All necessary measures were adopted to bring Jesus to consciousness. Otherwise what did Nicodemus mean by bringing the mixture of myrrh and aloes? . . . Joseph of Arimathea boldly asked the Governor to hand over the 'body' of Jesus which request he readily granted. If the plan was not pre-conceived, how could the Governor hand over the 'body' of Jesus to a stranger from the outside? There is reason to believe that Jesus Christ himself must have been informed of the plan so that his prophecy might come true that as Jonah was three days and three nights in the whale's belly so shall the Son of man be three days and three nights in the heart of the earth.

The soldiers did not break the legs of Jesus for they took him for a dead man and according to Hazrat Ahmad those soldiers 'incidentally pierced his side and forthwith there came out blood and water' which according to his group's belief is a 'surer sign of life for blood and water do not come out of a dead man's body'. The sect also points to the fact that due to the earthquake which ensued in Jerusalem people would 'hasten to go home' and there would be 'no one present on the scene who could definitely and certainly say that he saw Jesus "giving up the ghost".'

Jesus recovered and would then spend his remaining days – eighty-seven years! – fulfilling his mission to the 'lost sheep of Israel'. According to the sect's views, he would find them in Persia, Afghanistan and Kashmir and he was 'much more successful there than in Palestine'. Even the route taken by Jesus is known and the Ahmadiyyas point to Sprinager in Kashmir as the site of Jesus' tomb. This is based on the assumption that 'Yus Asaph', a prophet sent to the inhabitants of Kashmir, and Jesus are one and the same. According to the sect, the tomb is 'confirmed' by archaeological evidence but they refuse to have it opened as that would be contrary to Muslim law.

So far only the Ahmadiyya group of Muslims has shown an interest in the Shroud but one suspects that other Muslims may soon follow suit because all of Islam shares the conviction that Jesus did not die on the cross. The fourth chapter of the Koran is quite explicit on this point: '. . . yet they slew him not, neither crucified him, but he was represented by one in his likeness . . . They did not really kill him; but God took him up into himself . . .' There have been a variety of interpretations to remove Jesus from the death of the cross among Muslims. In George Sale's translation of the Koran he states: 'The real person crucified some thought to have been a spy that was sent to entrap (Jesus). Others thought that it was one Titian, who by the direction of Judas entered in at a window of the house where Jesus was, to kill him, and others that it was Judas himself, who agreed with the rulers of the Jews to betray him for thirty pieces of silver.'

Rodney Hoare, Senior Lecturer at Trent Polytechnic, has emerged as the latest author to entertain the argument that does not seem to go away – that Jesus survived the cross. According to his *The Testimony of the Shroud*, Hoare gave Shroud photographs to the East Midlands Forensic Laboratory in Nottingham to study. The forensic scientists reported that 'there was one feature which they could not equate with a normal dead body: the evenness of the stains'. They quoted a case that had occurred recently: 'A woman had died soon after getting out of her bath, and her naked body had fallen

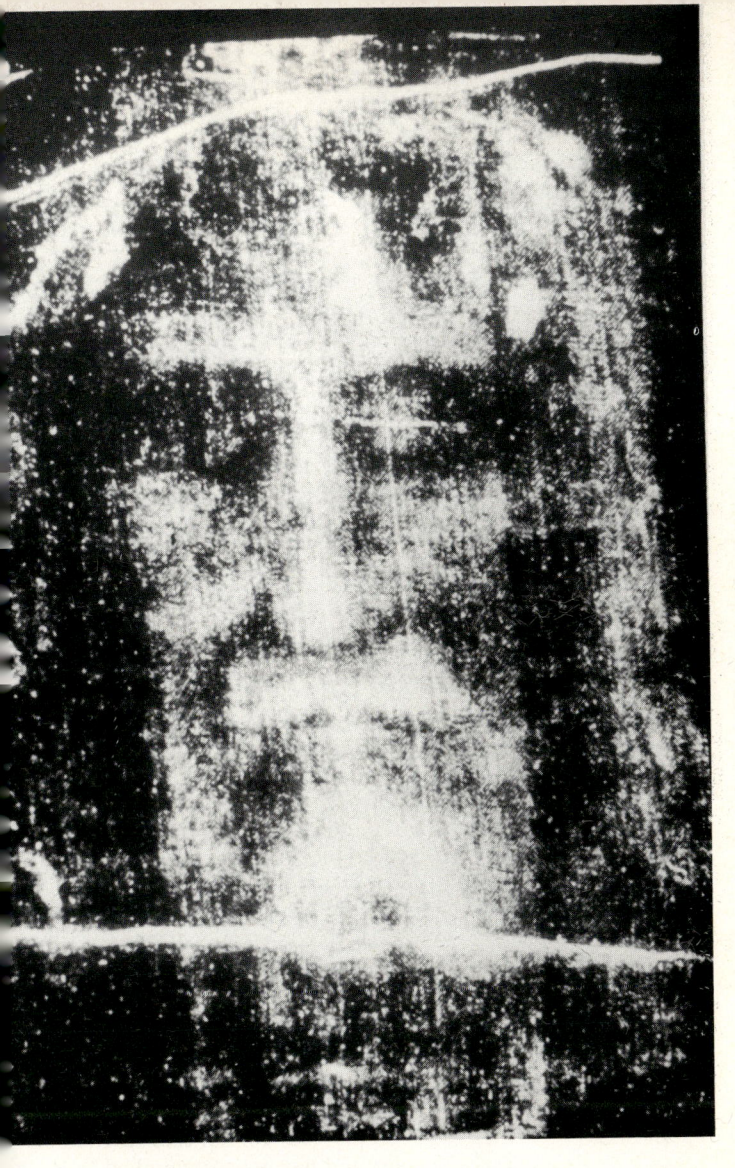

The face on the Shroud, as revealed by a negative plate.
Photograph taken by Giuseppe Enrie in 1931.

Fifth-century crucifixion scene on an ivory box.
(Courtesy of the British Museum).

The Savoyard Royal Chapel where the Shroud is normally kept.

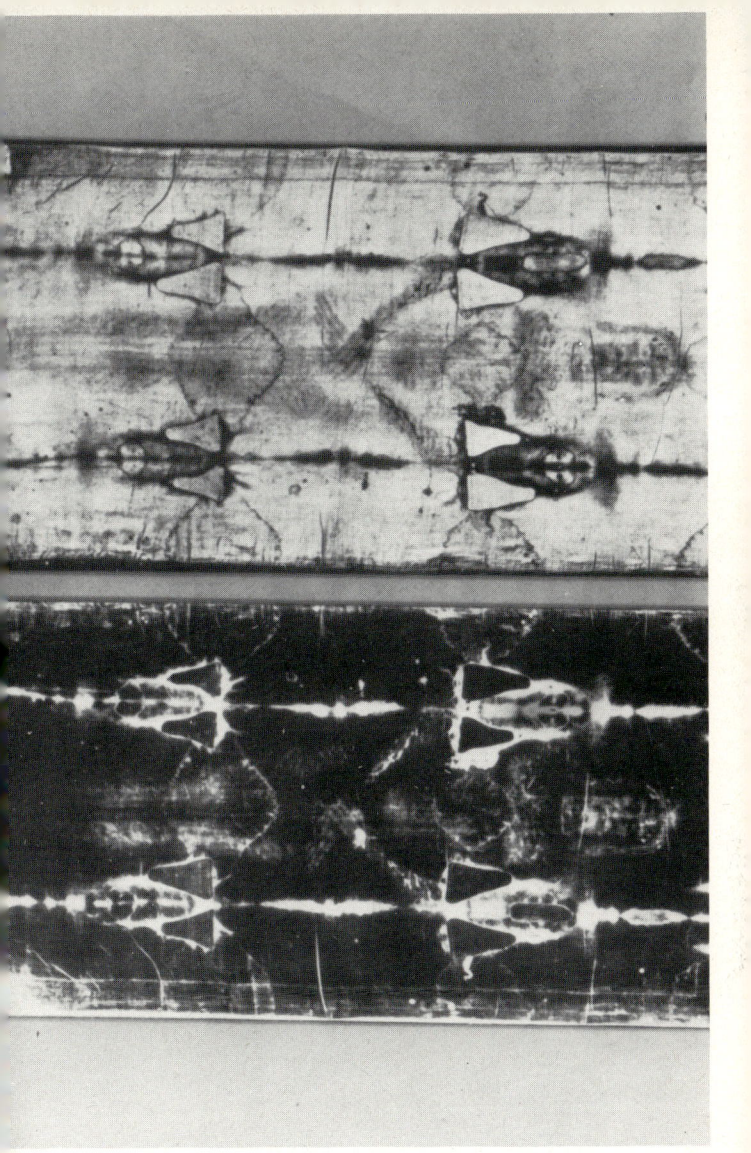

The full-length image on the Turin Shroud, both positive and negative. Photographs taken by Giuseppe Enrie in 1931.

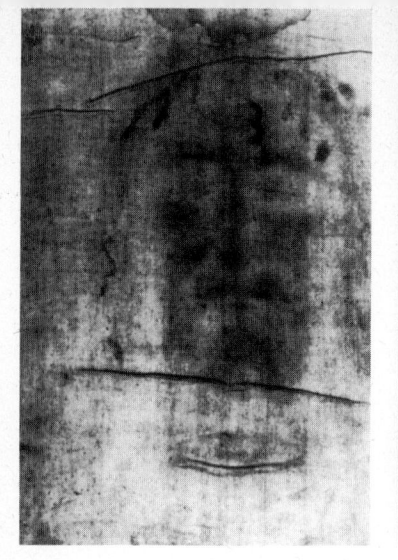

The face on the Shroud
Negative and positive plates
as photographed by Giuseppe Enrie in 1931.

Magnification of hand region, showing wound in wrist.

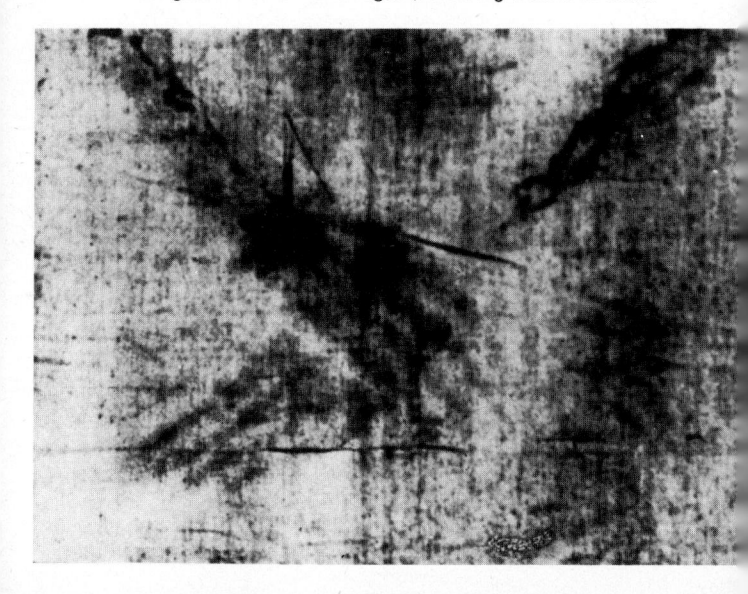

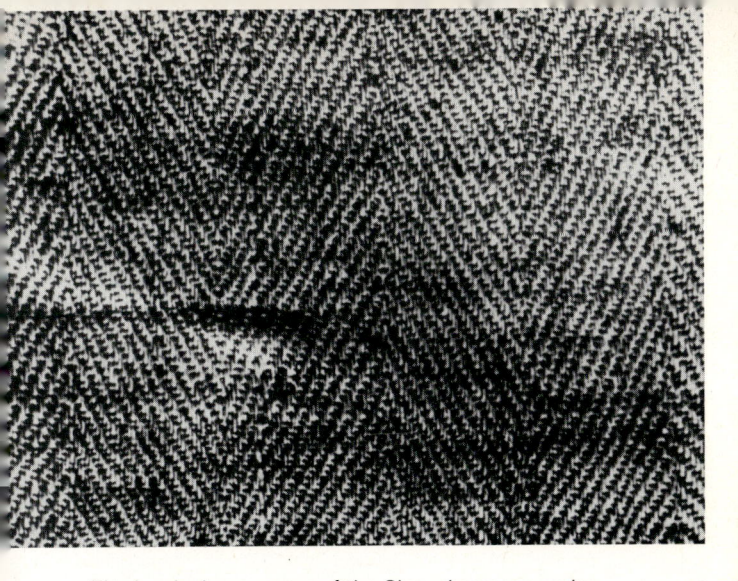

The herringbone weave of the Shroud as seen under magnification.

Leo Vala putting final touches to his three-dimensional screen of the Holy Face. *(Courtesy of Leo Vala)*

Captains John Jackson and Eric Jumper with the VP-8 Analyser. *(Courtesy of Screenpro Films Ltd)*

Relief image of the face on the Shroud produced by Jumper and Jackson through the VP-8 Analyser.

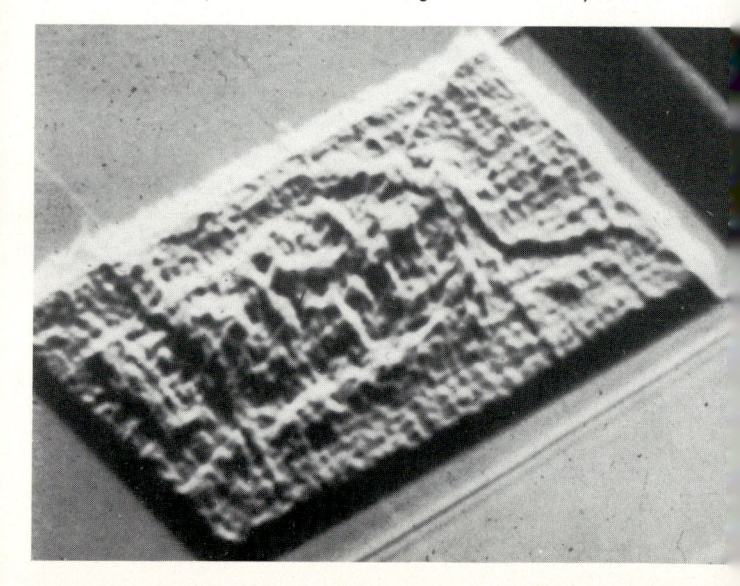

Three-dimensional model of the Turin Shroud figure made by Captains John Jackson and Eric Jumper.
(Courtesy of John Jackson)

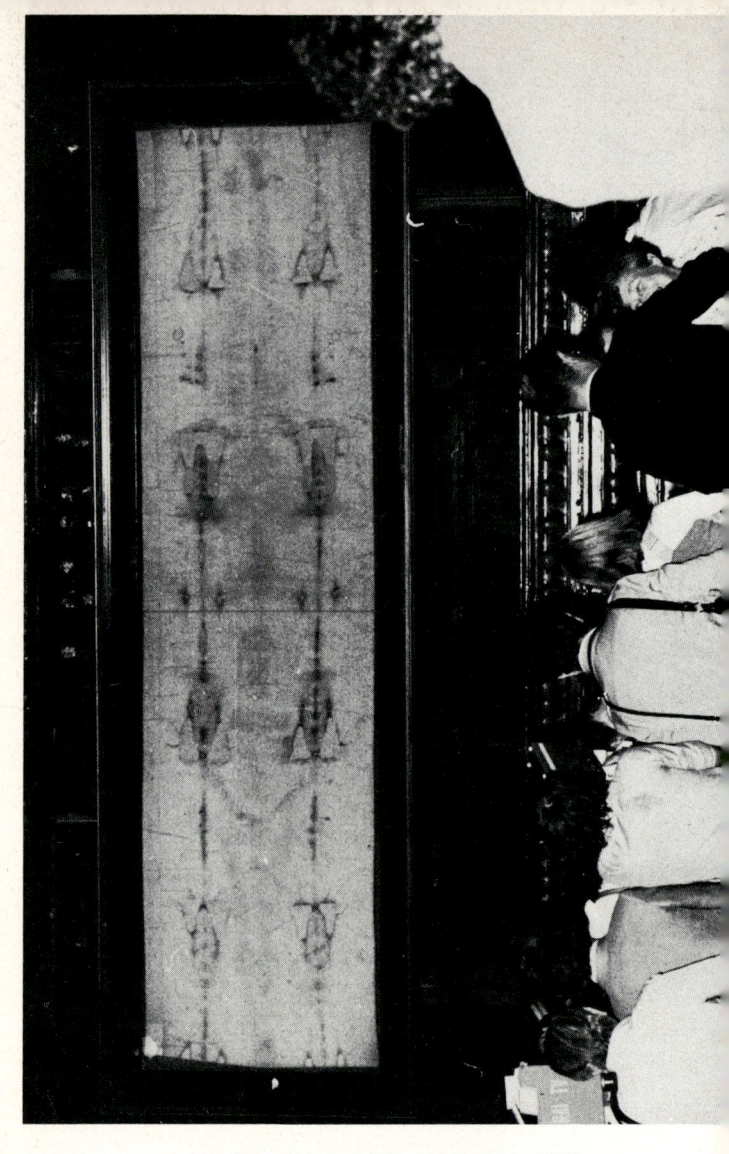

The Shroud as exhibited in Turin in 1978.
(Courtesy of La Stampa)

partly across the tiled bathroom floor and partly across the carpeted floor alongside. Such was the temperature difference quickly established, that by the time she was found half of her body was almost black with decomposition while the rest was still white'. This led Hoare to suggest, 'The evenness of the stains in the Shroud is therefore a problem.'[56] But he would go further.

Taking this theory that the lance thrust might not have been fatal, and checking Gray's *Anatomy* to see that *rigor mortis* 'sets in between three and six hours after death', Hoare reached another theory of Jesus surviving crucifixion. Jesus had lost consciousness and sunk into a comatose state, only appearing to be dead to those who would not know the difference. He was buried in this state and after three or four weeks recovered from his injuries. Hoare feels that the Shroud 'evidence' could give a 'plausible rational solution to the Resurrection' which he sees as so alien a concept to 'normal physical experience that they (would-be believers) cannot accept it, and so a whole-hearted allegiance to Christianity is not possible'. Therefore, if the body was still alive, resurrection could be explained as recovery.

Like the Ahmadiyya Muslims, Hoare involves the Gospel characters in new roles; Joseph of Arimathea and Nicodemus are the most likely candidates for the removal of Jesus' body from the tomb. 'They were followers of Jesus, but would not have been familiar with the main disciples who founded the Church and contributed to the gospels. The Church could not have been built on a guilty secret.' These two also had a reason for returning to the tomb – to finish their job of preparing Jesus' unwashed body for proper Jewish burial. Nicodemus and Joseph would have had no motive up to this point for removing the body until they entered the tomb and noticed 'probably . . . faint signs of breathing'. The two 'took the body to one of their houses to recover – likely Nicodemus's rather than Joseph's since he was not under the same suspicion – and their positions would have meant they would have kept the secret to themselves and perhaps one or two others whom they could trust implicitly'.

As with similar theorists, Hoare creates new problems with his 'rational' solution. The time of the Resurrection appearances has to be changed from three days to three weeks and the supernatural element in the reports of these appearances has to be rationalised to fit a 'recovered' Jesus. This school of thought therefore demands a rather loose interpretation of the gospels; 'The recollection of time is distorted by time' on the part of those who compiled them. Hoare reinforces his theory with some very arguable points: 'The survival of Jesus may have depended quite largely on the choice of centurion, and the right man had been chosen.' Judas is avenged by his theory and becomes 'the one Jesus trusted most'.

Hoare's ideas fall even more decidedly on his use of the Shroud as his chief evidence and he leaves no doubt as to its importance; 'We need a faith that will move mountains, and more and more people are looking to religion to provide an answer. The Shroud could help in this. Its purpose is to unify, not to divide; to confirm a new faith rather than to knock an old one.' Hoare feels that not only would the Jews be exonerated from their guilt of killing Jesus but 'Muslims, who believe Jesus to have been a great prophet of God, will no longer need to be offended by dogmatic Christian insistence on his divinity.'

Despite these magnanimous feelings, Rodney Hoare has some serious problems with his use of the Shroud as a proof for his theory. As has been previously noted, medical experts have suggested that there were enough reasons for Jesus to die without having the lance wound seen as a death blow. Jesus was already in a weakened condition from his experience in the Garden of Gethsemane. As pathologist, Robert Bucklin has written, 'It was in the Garden that the passion really began, and here it was that Christ suffered the bloody sweat' which it has been suggested was the phenomenon known as *haemohydrosis* (rupture of the capillaries caused by severe mental anguish – haemorrhage into the sweat glands). Christopher McManus has enumerated the important physiological effects of the scourging which would follow the next day.

The question of *rigor mortis* in the image of the man in the Shroud was faced at a talk delivered by the Home Office pathologist, Professor James Cameron, at the London Hospital Medical College 23 June 1978. Cameron unreservedly stated his view that the image showed that *rigor mortis* was to be seen throughout the body which had all the appearances of a dead man. Writing earlier, Robert Bucklin had said, 'The stiffness could have come only from *rigor mortis* and that means death is present – unless one wants to speculate on some sort of cataleptic state . . . (but) from the circumstances of the crucifixion, this would appear to be such a remote consideration that no one would think twice about it.' Bucklin has examined hundreds of corpses in his role as chief pathologist first at Los Angeles County and now at Austin, Texas. Bucklin's view of the evidence Hoare gives concerning the Nottingham woman was strong. 'I was particularly shocked at his comparison to the body of the woman . . . He describes post-mortem changes which are limited to only one part of the body, and he suggests that there was an element of decay. There is no evidence of decay as far as the body of the Man in the Shroud is concerned . . . As a pathologist, I would have no hesitancy in expressing a simple opinion that the image on the Shroud is that of a dead man. I believe the burden of proof of anything to the contary would be on the proponent of the opposite view.[57]

Most viewers who contend that Jesus did not die on the cross and use the Shroud as the evidence for that opinion are assuming that the images were caused by an ordinary contact process which as we will see in the next chapter was challenged by some important observations made in Albuquerque, New Mexico in 1977 by an unusual gathering of scientists.

CHAPTER 6

WHAT DID SCIENTISTS SAY ABOUT THE SHROUD 1969–1977?

Cardinal Pellegrino gave an inteview about the 1969 examination to a reporter of Radio Luxembourg. It was brief and fairly vague, ending with the remark that, 'There are no results as yet; the experts have not had time to examine their analyses.'

Even the Shroud's legal owner, ex-King Umberto II, was unaware of just what had taken place, and was being planned. The only semi-official word he received was the private communication by a friend who had been on the Cardinal's commission of experts. The attitude of Turin's religious establishment concerning the Shroud has been very difficult to understand. Part of the difficulty stems from the awkward matter of ownership. Legally and technically it is the property of the House of Savoy in the person of Umberto. His father, Victor Emmanuel III, was forced to abdicate in 1946 by the Allied Powers. Umberto reigned in his own right only a month, leaving Italy for exile after a plebiscite on the monarchy gave a small majority to the republicans in June 1946. In this democratic fashion one of the oldest royal houses in Europe ceased to rule. Umberto moved to Villa Italia in Cascais, Portugal, a comfortable house in an area once highly populated by other ex-monarchs of Europe and their families. The King, a slim and elegant leader of the dwindling set of aristocrats, has been a shrewd businessman with substantial holdings in England, and most of his wealth is due to his own efforts while in exile. Umberto's family situation has not been the same success[58] and friends close to him have hinted for years that he was considering willing the Savoyard patronage of the dynasty to the cadet line in the person of the popular Duke of Aosta, Amadeus, who is married to the daughter of the Count of Paris. This situation vitally affects the future of the Shroud. The Italian state has been slowly confiscating the property of the House of Savoy piece by piece. Several years ago there was a great fuss over the crown jewels, the sale of which some saw as possibly aiding the serious economic problems of Italy. Rumours circulated that some of the jewels were missing from their Bank of Italy safekeeping. An inspection was made; the jewels were intact but their value was nothing like what was needed to help the economy. What will happen to them no one knows but the Italian treasury made it clear that it felt they belonged to the State over Umberto's insistence that they are family property. He views the Shroud in a similar manner but before he went into exile he designated the Archbishop of Turin as the day-to-day custodian of the relic. The ownership of the Shroud is also complicated by the fact that it is housed in the 'Royal Chapel' of the old Savoyard palace now owned by the State. This chapel is physically part of the Cathedral but technically a separate entity.

In the five times I have talked with the ex-King he has displayed a concern for the relic's future and has confided that he will leave it to the Vatican at his death in order to solve its legal status. Umberto has also shown a keen interest in the Shroud's possible testing in the past several years. This was not always the case. He inherited his father's reticence as regards investigations of its complexities. Following the 1931 exposition, King Victor Emmanuel adopted an attitude that those who refused to believe in the authenticity of the relic after the astounding re-confirmation of its unique photographic qualities, would not be convinced by new evidence made possible by various tests. Umberto changed his attitude but many in Turin did not change with him. They still gave the fact of Savoyard ownership as an excuse for not having direct scientific testing.

By his own admission, Michele Pellegrino was never vitally interested in the Shroud; his concerns were centred in the perplexing social problems of Turin with its expanding population. One reliable story has it that in 1968 when Pope Paul VI appointed him as Archbishop of Turin, he asked what he saw were the top priorities for his new post. Pellegrino responded that first he must be concerned with the some 300,000 emigrants who had settled into the area of Turin from the south of Italy. Secondly would be the care of his fellow priests. 'And one more – one more must be added,' responded the Pope. 'That must be the Shroud of Turin.' The pressure for getting anything done has almost always come from outside Turin. It is said that the idea for the 1973 television exposition (with its important attendant tests) came from Father Rinaldi, and it was Pope Paul who gently but decidedly moved Turin into its acceptance. With his death there will probably be some interesting revelations as to just how firmly committed Paul VI was to the investigations on the Shroud. He surprised all those in charge in Turin by insisting that he appear on the television programme. He spoke of the great impression that the cloth made upon him when he saw it in 1931: '. . . so true, so profound, so human, so divine'.

The popes have never formally pronounced the Turin Shroud to be genuine, although they have over the years sanctioned its veneration over against the claims of other 'shrouds'. Of the modern pontiffs, Pius XI displayed the most profound regard for it: as a scholar he was convinced of its authenticity and as a spiritual leader it was this image which he most often gave to bishops and others received in audience. Seven days before his death, the Cardinal Archbishop of Quebec and other Canadian bishops visiting him received pictures of the Shroud's face from him with his feeling that they represented the true likeness of Christ. Pius XI had received Giuseppe Enrie, Paul Vignon and Pierre Barbet in audiences and the last public exposition in 1933 was held at his own request.

King Umberto's arrangement of having the Turin Archbishop as the custodian officially meant that the latter could take whatever initiative he judged necessary with, of course, the approval of the Pope and the King. In practice, this has not worked out so easily. There has always been a core of conservative clergy in Turin who have effectively stymied scientific investigation. Monsignor Jose Cottino, Cardinal Pellegrino's choice of 'overseer of Shroud matters', did not make it very easy to obtain accurate information. It appeared that nothing had been planned for the relic other than a routine examination to ascertain its present-day condition and that the idea behind the television programme was solely 'to increase devotion to the Shroud by showing it to as many people as possible'. No hint was given that following this exposition there was to be a second round of investigations.

On Friday, 23 November 1973 about 100 million Europeans viewed the Shroud on television. Hanging upright in a massive but unadorned frame with no protective glass, the Shroud was laid open to the strong television lights. The programme was overly devotional in tone and there was no attempt to discuss the scientific aspects of the curious images. The authorities in Turin had decided not to let any possible controversy mar what they called the 'religiousness' of the event.

There was no word from Turin for almost three years as to what had occurred the day following the televising. 3 March 1976, on BBC Radio 4's programme, 'Sunday', would be the first time most individuals in this country would have a hint of the investigations. The programme gave the news that Max Frei of Zurich had removed pollen from the cloth in 1973 and 'was able to verify that there were specks of pollen present from Constantinople . . . and from plants known to have grown in Palestine some twenty centuries ago'. Clive Jacobs also reported that the Turin Commission results 'were due last September but today the Church has published nothing despite the fact that a number of leaks about the findings have found their way into the press'. One of the people most anxious to see those findings in Britain, Dr David Willis, died on Palm Sunday, 1976, in the middle of taping his reactions to the scattered reports of the tests before he was able to see the published report. Earlier, Willis had given some astute observations on the situation:

> Will the day ever come when they (the Turin authorities) will realise that the Turin Shroud, in a broad sense, belongs to all Christianity, in fact to humanity itself? How can a relic of such tremendous significance be kept locked in a vault for decades at a time? And when finally brought to light, why is it examined secretly, without the competent authorities as much making an official statement that would obviate the confusing reports of press releases? . . . But this can all be corrected in the future by Cardinal Pellegrino resisting all temptations to secrecy and insisting on a *full-scale, open, legally attested, international, scientific investigation*. An Italian team acting in secrecy will convince no one.[59]

Willis' words were prophetic as we will see. Shortly after Willis' death, it was apparent from the Commission report (which had to be translated into English in this country) just what had occurred with the Shroud on 16–17 June 1969 and 22–23 November 1973. Resolutions at the 1939 and 1950 sindological congresses for direct scientific testing had gone unheeded until Cardinal Fossati's successor, Michele Pellegrino, began the slow machinery of assembling a list of commission experts. The first desire of the commission was to ascertain what, if any, harmful effects the increasing industrial pollution of Turin might be having upon the cloth. There were eleven official members of the group and all of them were Italian except the late addition of the Belgian Professor Gilbert Raes who was asked to examine the weave of the linen. Of the Italians, all save two were from Turin. This restriction to fairly 'local talent' meant that they would be able to go only so far considering the lack of scientific equipment at their disposal. The original objectives were much more far-reaching than they had indicated to the press: Ascertaining the probable dating of the cloth and patches; identifying the various substances present in the marks of different colour found on the cloth; examination of the whole sheet by various optical methods (photography, microphotography, chromatic and spectroscopic analysis); examination of the fabric itself and removal of minimal samples for 'microdetermination' of various kinds. As it turned out the commission members had to work within a very short period of examination time and there was almost no overall coordination of effort and intention. Professor Enzio Delorenzi would later tell me that when he arrived to complete his investigations as to the suitability of further radiological examination he would be told that the relic had already been returned to its reliquary and so his final written report would be an embarrassment since he really was not able to make a full conclusion. Aside from not working in concert and integrating the results of its efforts with previous findings and studies of the cloth, the commission was hampered by the exclusion of biblical exegesis, theology, history and, most important of all, pathology.

It is very easy to point out the limitations of the commission report and a *Critical Study* made under the auspices of the Sindonological Centre in Turin did a devastating job of that in 1977. But in fairness it should be pointed out that there were some unexpected things discovered and reported and this would mean there would be no turning back to the previous 'silent and secret' attitude in Turin. As Father Rinaldi put it, 'Even if Turin botched this first positive step by limiting the work of the commission and surrounding it with uncalled-for secrecy, it was a breakthrough of a sort.'[60]

Probably the most detailed and exhaustive report was given by the curator of the Egyptian Museum of Turin, Silvio Curto. In the several times I have talked with him, I found him to have a very open and academic attitude toward the Shroud. He had certainly done his 'homework' in his archaeological observations concerning the Shroud fabric and its images. In his conclusions he stated that the cloth 'may date back to the time of Christ' and the image is either 'authentic', due to some mechanical process working as a photograph at the time of the Deposition, or that of a 'model', '. . . artistically produced by some kind of printing technique . . . no earlier than the tenth century' (the latter was the idea of the only woman on the commission, Noemi Gabrielli – as we shall see). Curto completely rejected the possibility that any colouring substance whatsoever had impregnated the threads of the Shroud and mentioned the interesting information that the backing to the Shroud had been partially removed during examination. This plus other evidence led him to write, 'The image is completely superficial'. In private correspondence he went further, '. . . no grains of any impregnating material could be seen at the microscope . . .' (this referred to removed threads which will be discussed later). Curto described the colour of the blood as darker and brownish in comparison to the sepia-coloured body image. He was able to see two traces of a crimson colour which he felt 'must certainly have been added later and deliberately'. When I questioned him about this remark, he remembered them to be near the large wound in the side.

Professor Curto's initial impression of the fabric of the relic was that it was very similar to the linens of Pharaonic Egypt kept in his museum which are among the finest in the world. There was no problem with the size of the Shroud; Egyptian pieces of similar dimensions appeared in several archaeological findings. The Turin cloth measures approximately 4.36 x 1,203 metres and something not generally understood is that there is a strip sewn on one side which is about 15 cm wide. There is no agreement as to when this was added – some feel that it has been an integral part of the cloth from its beginning, but as Curto has suggested, '. . . it is easier to assume that it was added as a repair, because the image is across the middle of the entire Shroud'. The Shroud fabric is a twill (herringbone) weave as we have earlier noted, but the Egyptians from the time of the Pharaohs down to the Roman period always used a simpler weaving type – a plain weave with weft-threads passing alternately over and under one warp-thread, producing perpendicular lines. The Turin Shroud fabric presents diagonal lines of twill weaving with weft-threads passing alternately under one and over two or more warp-threads. Curto added, 'Very little is known about the origins of the twill weaving; suffice it to say that similar improvements of the art of weaving had been reported at the time of the Roman Empire. It is known that the bandages of mummies found in Antinoe (Hadrian's city in Egypt) were of the twill type and dated from between AD 136 and 200'[61] But as Curto concluded, '. . . this technique does not appear to have its origins in Egypt but rather Syria or Mesopotamia'. With Palestine at the cross-roads between the two centres it is not unusual to find both kinds of weaving plus some variations at the time of Christ.

Added to Curto's report was that of a colleague, Professor G. Raes, Director of Ghent University's textile laboratory. A very pragmatic analyser of textiles for academics and business, Raes was to have two fairly sizeable portions of the Shroud in his possession until November 1976. Three years earlier these samples (the larger – 110mg 5cm^2; the smaller – 70mg 3cm^2) were removed by nuns for fabric analysis at Professor Curto's suggestions. The larger was from the 'added' edge;[62] the smaller from the main body of the cloth. Raes discovered that both pieces were of the same herring-bone design of a similar raw linen, as were the sewing threads. It is well known that flax was grown in Palestine and that priestly garments and wrappers for sacred scrolls (as with the Dead Sea Scrolls) were of linen. The young man who broke away on the night of Jesus' arrest wore a fine linen cloth and linen was generally used to enshroud the dead. The sample taken from the main portion of the Shroud contained, however, traces of cotton, corresponding to the type, *Herbaceum*, known to have existed in the ancient Middle East. In ancient Egypt only pure linen was used; cotton had its origins in India, coming into use around the Mediterranean in the sixth century B.C. but not used in weaving until the Roman era. Both linen weft and warp threads pulled from the sample in question showed traces of cotton, indicating that the spinner used cotton as well as flax. Raes gave no explanation to this, apparently feeling that it was not very significant.

Yigael Yadin, an Israeli archaeologist of distinction, was

involved with the finding of a number of textiles in the important Bar Kokhba caves discoveries of 1960–61. They were dated to not later than AD 135 and of them Yadin stated, 'The clothing and other woven material showed that the weavers and wearers of them were very orthodox Jews. Not even once is there an occurrence of mixing diverse kinds of fibres, that is wool and linen or vice versa, as prohibited by the law of Moses.[63] The Mishnah makes it clear that cotton could be mixed with flax without there being any transgression. Yadin's group discovered a child's linen shirt which was in remarkably good condition, attesting to the fact that linen garments can survive a great deal of abuse.

It is clear in the Mishnah that cotton was allowed to be mixed with flax without there being any transgression of 'mixing of kinds' (this was not true of wool). Raes' concluding remark like so many others to be found in the report was extremely noncommittal, 'On the basis of the . . . observations we can say that we have no precise indication that the fabric *does not* date back to the time of Christ. But on the other hand, it is also not possible to confirm that the fabric in question *has*, in fact, been woven in that period of time.'

The Waldensian Protestant Director of Modena University's Institute of Legal Medicine, Professor Giorgio Frache, was in charge of the haematological investigations. Eleven threads of varying lengths were made available for Frache's use under a stereoscopic microscope. The longest contained no image; two had 'scourge marks' and the remainder possessed 'blood' markings. All the samples had been extracted from the Shroud by four sisters of the Turin Institute of the Daughters of St Joseph who were experts in darning and embroidery. The removal of the threads was undertaken with the sole aid of a fine needle 'by means of which a thread was isolated where the experts indicated, and extracted with a light tug'. Frache's first examination showed the fibres to be of a shiny honey colour and at the level of impregnation with the 'blood stains' only the very surface fibres took on a fairly uniform reddish colour. That colouring was located in the surface fibres 'so much so that the reddish colouring was only observed on the reverse of the thread at the level of the underlying fibres by transparency'. Next Frache and his assistants proceeded with several chemical tests searching for haemoglobin residues. A persistent component of blood, peroxidase, was searched for with the use of benzidine which would have turned the stain a characteristic blue, but that did not occur. The microspectroscopic and thin-layer chromatography gave negative results as well. Frache's report was preceded with a warning that testing for blood on ancient linen created problems, '. . . the specific protein of blood and related pigmentation, if subjected for various reasons to processes of denaturisation, may well lose the characteristics which permit identification.' Some writers had previously suggested that the heat of the 1532 fire could have rendered non-active any haemoglobin possibly present on the linen. This investigation concurred with Curto's observation that there is a complete absence of any pigments on the Shroud.

Two anatomists from Turin, Guido Filogamo and Alberto Zina, conducted microscopic investigations on threads removed from the cloth to find out if there were any traces of haematic origin (red globules). Their examinations did not reveal corpuscles but the ultrastructural analysis showed that what did appear was made up of amorphous material with no specific differential. 'The possibility that formations of this kind may be red globules cannot be excluded with absolute certainty . . .' was one of the conclusions plus the interesting remark that 'more significant data might be furnished from a study of the threads under a scanning electron microscope' (unfortunately not available to them).

Dr Cesare Codegone of the Turin Polytechnic Institute had the task of advising about the possibility of radiocarbon dating the relic. The Committee were still unaware that carbon dating processes no longer made it necessary to use such a large sample as in the method developed by Dr Willard F. Libby of the University of Chicago about twenty years ago. That original test would require a handkerchief size sample – something no authorities would allow in the case of the Shroud.

Professor Neomi Gabrielli, the retired director of the Art Galleries of Piedmont, suggested the view that the Shroud '. . . is the work of a great artist of the late fifteenth century and early sixteenth centuries, who used the Leonardo technique of shading . . . If we compare the Shroud with the face of Christ in the "Last Supper" we find a similarity of technique and spirituality.' Gabrielli felt that the image could not have been painted but pointed to the possibility that the article was probably printed: the artist first designed the picture on cloth using sepia and ochre mixed with a resin solution. He then spread this cloth with its original design still wet on a shroud, pressing it gently – possibly with a soft, surfaced weight. Despite this 'solution' she admitted to the difficulties presented by the extraordinary anatomical perfection of the image.

The third photographer of the Shroud would be Giovanni Battista Judica-Cordiglia, who took his shots during the investigations of 18 June 1969. He had large equipment for the event: studio camera 7 with plates size 10.7 x 12.7 cm. by the Lupo firm; Mamya Professional C.220; Exakta 24 x 36 mm.; Osram Nitaphot lamps with a total of 8,000 watts. Having shot several photographs in black and white and also in colour, and using various time exposures (from 1/5 of a second to nine seconds) Judica-Cordiglia felt certain of obtaining some first-rate negatives. Only the result of the colour was good; the others were disappointing as he admitted:

The first black and white copy was ready towards the evening and our surprise was great when we saw that the reproduced image didn't appear as 'engraved' as in Enrie's pictures but weaker and paler . . . as if the plates were underexposed, even if we had had different exposures . . . However . . . the negatives appeared correctly exposed. Being used to observing the pictures by Enrie, one could nevertheless notice a baffling difference in the reproduction of the details. We thought at once that the latter had 'doubleprinted' the image to emphasize the contrast.

Doubleprinting is a method frequently used to heighten contrast – duplicating the first negative onto a second one with different shades. There is no doubt that Enrie did not use this method. As has been stated earlier, he was surrounded by photographic experts (including Pia) throughout every step of his work. Ezio and Elio Dutto, who took over Enrie's studio in 1939 have stressed that the equipment used by the first two photographers and their methods are the reason for the difference:

> Reproduction by means of plates come out much more sharp in print than the ones obtained through films ... The emulsions of Pia's and Enrie's plates were less sensitive, therefore they had to use long exposures – for Enrie nine minutes for some and two for others; while for Judica-Cordiglia the longest time had been nine seconds. The exposure, though correct and suitable for colour film, was not the reason for the modest result. Quite simply, orthochromatic plates with low sensitivity (an emulsion non-chemically active to the colour red and therefore not very sensitive to warm tonalities) were the reason why Enrie achieved a good contrast of images.

The Turin Shroud, as can be clearly seen with the colour photographs, is a study of warm tones. Others have stressed the importance of Pia's and Enrie's big plates, the greater distance of their shots and the use of optics with long and diaphragmed distances as reasons for the differences in the 1931 and 1969 results. It was unfortunate that the advice given that several rather than one photographer be used was not heeded.

The most exciting outcome of the commission investigations as far as press reaction was concerned came from someone who was not an official member of the group of experts, Dr Max Frei of Zurich. A criminologist of some repute (he assisted in the 1961 investigations of Dag Hammarskjold's death) and an evangelical Protestant, Frei had been called to Turin with two other experts to notarise Judica-Cordiglia's photographs in 1973. While studying the weave of the

Shroud with enlargements of these photographs, Frei noticed minute dust particles between the linen threads. He proposed an examination of these tiny grains. Using a special adhesive tape pressed gently against the cloth, Frei removed twelve samples mainly from the border, avoiding the image, during the nights of 23 and 24 November. He took his 'collection' back to his Zurich laboratory with its powerful stereoscopic and scanning electron microscopes, comparing the gathered pollen with an infinite amount of possibilities. Pollen analysis has been an acknowledged archaeological technique for some time. The pollen of every variety of plant can be distinguished separately under the microscope because each has a particular shape and dimension, a variety of pores and grooves and varying structures in the outer wall. The shell is preserved dry with all of its details for centuries without any changes even if the pollen is found in ice or mud or at the bottom of lakes, and it penetrates everywhere, as hay fever sufferers well know! It is an almost perfect clue. For twenty-five years, Frei worked with the Zurich police mapping the comings and goings of criminals using the telltale pollen as an invaluable tool for detection. Studying the pollen from the suspect's garments or weapons, a map of his travels, his presence at the scene of the crime or the place of storing evidence can be determined.

With his samples from the Shroud, Frei felt that it was possible, therefore, to chart the travels of the relic by identifying the origin of the various grains he had in his possession. This was not to be an easy task as he stated:

When I began my studies on the Shroud in 1973 in my relatively restrained spare time I never imagined that I would be obliged to travel personally several times to Palestine, Anatolia, Cyprus, France and Italy in different seasons, but this revealed itself to be absolutely necessary, because reference-collections of pollen very rarely contain samples of desert plants or plants of the steppes and even herbarium specimens which I consulted, very often had not been collected at the exact moment when the pollen was mature for propagation. Thus I travelled myself to these countries . . .

Frei has studied more than one thousand specimens of pollen, especially those relying on the wind for pollination since the Shroud was known to have been exposed in the open air and linen was frequently woven out of doors in the Near East. He has been able to isolate more than fifty different pollen species – some as expected were from the region around Turin and central France. A significant number were from Palestine and the Anatolian steppes of Turkey but no particular Cypriot species were found. He has been able to verify the existence of certain Palestinian specimens with pollen known to have existed two thousand years ago by comparing them with microfossils in alluvia in the Jordan Valley and on the bottom of the Lake of Galilee. Some of the Palestinian finds correspond to common plants which have remained the same from New Testament days. The flora of the steppes of Anatolia have not undergone fundamental changes in two thousand years according to Frei. In his customary self-assured manner, he has been able to conclude, 'My findings must be interpreted as a valid proof for the fact that the Shroud of Turin during its history was exposed to the open air in Palestine and Turkey.'[64]

Cesare Codegone had advised against the carbon-14 dating test for the Shroud thinking that a large sample was still required. It never seemed to occur to anyone on the commission that the two samples removed for Professor Raes' fabric study could be so used. By 1976 the sample weight required had gone from approximately 40 grams to 60 milligrams; the sample area from 40 x 40 centimetres to 1/20 of that area. This meant that Raes' samples would fall easily within the new range. A number of friends in England and America were aware of this possibility and I decided to find out where the samples were in July of 1976 during a trip to Turin. Several experts in carbon dating had provided me with the necessary data on the new tests.

Finding the samples was not an easy task. By this time however, the names of the commission of experts were known so I started hunting for corresponding addresses in the local telephone book. Monsignor Cottino, who was still acting as the Cardinal's spokesman on matters related to the Shroud was certain that the samples were in the reliquary of the Royal Chapel. Others felt they had been destroyed, but one commission member, Silvio Curto, knew exactly where they were. They had remained in the possession of Gilbert Raes in his flat in Ghent for three years. I wrote to Raes upon my return from Turin and explained the new carbon dating tests. He was keenly interested and ended his reply with a sentence any C-14 laboratory would relish reading: 'I should like to know how to proceed for the forwarding of the samples.'

None of us interested in this possibility expected a test to ensue immediately. Fortunately a microanalyst from Chicago, Walter McCrone, who knew a great deal about the new tests was in London at this time. McCrone is best known for his debunking the Vinland Map, which indicated a pre-Columbian mapping of the New World. His laboratory has analysed a number of important pieces of art which has brought it into close contact with radiocarbon dating centres. McCrone had a portable set of miscroscopes with him when Professor Raes produced the Shroud samples in his dining room. We were surprised to find them kept in a rather casual manner in an old scrap-book of stamps. Also surprising was their excellent condition; a routine check showed them to be entirely suitable for carbon dating.

Dr McCrone and I were unaware that Professor Raes had been in touch with a carbon-14 expert from the University of Louvain-La-Neuve, Professor Désiré Apers. At this time Walter McCrone was proposing a method of carbon dating using 'nuclear track emulsions'. This method was never accepted fully in Europe (and has been generally discarded throughout the world) and Apers' physics analysis of it in relationship to the Shroud was devastating.

It would take some time to produce a better test proposal and during this period of reconsideration Professor Raes decided to take my advice and be in touch with the Turin authorities about the samples' future retention. Turin's answer was a firm request that the professor return them immediately which he did – by post! They were then placed in the sacristy vault of the Royal Chapel where they still remain.

The *Sunday Times* interviewed the custodian of the Royal Chapel, Monsignor Pietro Caramello, for an Easter Day 1977 article on the Shroud and in response to a query about the possibility of carbon dating the Shroud he seemed to indicate that no pieces were ever cut from the relic.[65] I had just returned from a visit to King Umberto at this time and in a letter to the editor the following Sunday I expressed the King's interest in the test possibility and gave the page and photograph references to the removed samples in the Turin Commission report in which the Monsignor is listed as the chairman of the group.

Shortly after Fathers Rinaldi and Otterbein of the American Holy Shroud Guild returned to the States following the 1973 television exposition, they were contacted by a twenty-seven year old Air Force captain and physicist, John Jackson, about an entirely new scientific approach towards understanding the Shroud images that he and an equally youthful colleague, Eric Jumper, were making during their free time from classes at the Air Force Weapons Laboratory in Albuquerque, New Mexico. Using a sophisticated instrument known as the VP-Image Analyser, the two discovered that the Turin Shroud is naturally third-dimensional.

Ever since Pia's 1898 photographing, it had been noted that the image darkness on the Shroud varies from point to point suggesting a process acting over a distance. Paul Vignon had observed that the image seemed to be present even where the cloth could not have touched the body. The closer the body was to the cloth the darker the image. To ascertain if there were a mathematically quantifiable relationship between the image intensities on the Shroud and the distances it must have been from the body, Jackson and Jumper made a cloth model of the relic marking the various points in colour code: red indicated the 'blood' stains, black the 'body' images, orange the Chambery burn marks and so on. With the model Shroud, the two captains were able to wrap eleven cadet volunteers to find a matching body type. The cadet who best corresponded to the marked cloth was a hairy 175 lb. young man whose height was 5 ft. 10 in. – almost exactly what anatomists had previously calculated for the man of the Shroud. With the proper 'subject' it was a simple matter to next measure the distance various portions of the marked cloth were from the subject beneath. A microdensitometer, which measures image intensities on photographic transparencies, was employed to measure the density of corresponding locations on the image by scanning the 1931 Enrie photographs. The results of the experiments showed that Vignon's observations were correct and could be scientifically charted.[66]

Jackson and Jumper's assumption that a body enshrouded in the cloth had produced the image on it was scientifically provable. They stressed the importance of this image analysis for the future of Shroud studies. Image analysis is able to provide a mathematical measurement of any image's properties. An exact measurement, of just how sharp and how rough edges are, can be calculated. The computer image analysis made it possible to transform visual information into a set of numerical values, and the resulting curve they discovered represented the first mathematical means of testing the various theories about how the image was formed. The two stressed the importance of this mathematical discovery: '. . . whenever a subject can be placed in a mathematical context, increased knowledge of that subject quickly follows. After all, mathematics is the language of science. We cannot help but observe that the relationship between image intensity and cloth-body distance is a mathematical characteristic of the Shroud image.'

When Jackson and Jumper first viewed the VP-8 Analyser's three-dimensional portrait of the Shroud they said they knew how Secondo Pia must have felt on looking into his 1898 negative plate. The Shroud not only has the properties of a photographic negative but is three-dimensional in character, a quality unheard of in the history of art or photography. Ordinary photographs do not have this property – transformed into vertical relief they will present obvious distortion with noses pushed into faces and arms into chests. To obtain the '3-D' photographs we see on post cards and in special effects, at least two photographs are required, separated by a known distance. In the case of the Shroud, the resulting three-dimensional portraits presented a natural, proportioned body lacking any apparent distortion.

According to the two scientists this means:

1. The image formation was uniform and independent of body surface qualities.
2. The lay of the Shroud was relatively flat.
3. Processes tending to change image intensity acted uniformly or not at all. Since no distortion exists when the Shroud image is transformed into vertical relief, its three-dimensionality must be a distinctive characteristic.

It seemed unlikely then that the image had been produced by direct contact. This would have caused the image to appear flat-topped with all areas of contact having the same vertical elevation. The three-dimensional image of the Shroud showed that the image forming process acted similarly on the top and bottom sides of the body. The hair on the frontal image stood out in natural relief, but on the back it appeared compressed against the head, as it would for a reclining body on a hard surface. The calves of the legs seemed proportionally rounded as did the ankles on the front image. The front and back images, therefore, had nearly the same maximum elevation, implying equal contact intensities.

Jackson and Jumper also reported in *Science* magazine (21 July 1978) that, 'The water marks and numerous small intense features on the body have abrupt edges, whereas the large burn marks have smoothly decaying edges. This suggests a different mechanism of formation for the two types of features . . . Analysis of the facial region revealed that the image is composed of a wide range of spatial frequencies which are oriented in a random fashion. This indicates that the feature-generating mechanism was probably directionless . . .' This latter observation was reinforced by another scientist as we will see and indicates a characteristic not consistent with a hand application.

An interesting sidelight to these discoveries was the ability to construct a lifesize 'sculpture' of the Shroud figure. Jackson and Jumper made body profile 'slices' by electronically scanning the photographic image, ascertaining the density for each and then reproducing these pieces on 570 sheets of cardboard. These were assembled to form an impressive figure.

Relief enhancement of a close-up of the Shroud face revealed an interesting possibility – what appeared as two 'button-like' or 'coin-shaped' objects resting over the eyes. They clearly protruded over the eye-section of an otherwise reasonable facial structure. This led Jackson and Jumper to speculate that they might indicate a burial practice of placing coins or similar objects over the deceased's eyelids. This is a known custom among various peoples but investigation as to its being a practice among the Jews of Jesus' day has been disappointing. The only reference yet uncovered is rather oblique. In the 1894–95 edition of the *Jewish Quarterly Review*, A. P. Bender writing on Jewish burial customs, referred to a statement by anthropologist, Sir James Frazer, that 'The Jews put a potsherd and the Russians coins on each of the eyes.' There is no doubt from this article that there has always been a certain importance attached to the closing of the deceased's eyes among the Jews: 'As man is supposed to behold the Shechina in the moment he expires, it is not proper that his eyes rest upon a profane object after this vision . . .' But with the Jews as with other ancient peoples, we are in the realm of folklore when it comes to the exactitudes of practice, about which precious little documentation exists. Despite this, the two scientists feel that newer close-up photographs might identify the objects and, if they be coins, it would be a truly unique dating process![67]

Another unexplained phenomenon is the presence of an obvious 'bulge' over the forehead of the figure. It has been suggested that this might indicate the phylactery which goes around the head of a Jewish man. Phylacteries are small square leather boxes containing passages from the Torah and used during morning weekday prayers. Recent excavations at the Dead Sea Qumran 'Grotte 4' unearthed remains of phylacteries roughly from the time of Christ. The scripture-containing boxes of that time were not as 'boxlike' as modern equivalents and the experts I talked with in Jerusalem and Qumran discounted the possibility of burial with the objects.

Jackson and Jumper felt that they had discovered strong arguments in favour of the authenticity of the Turin relic: 'We submit that an artist or forger living then (fourteenth century) would not have been able to encode three-dimensional information by adjusting the intensity levels of his work to everywhere correspond to actual cloth-body separations.' Shroud studies had entered the space age and what had started out as fairly casual exploratory experiments would initiate a very advanced scientific investigation into the image creation process. Rinaldi and Otterbein went to Albuquerque in Febrary 1976 to see the work of Jackson and Jumper and plans were started for the first United States Conference on the Shroud of Turin.

The two captains accepted new postings at the United States Air Force Academy at Colorado Springs near Denver where they would interest other military scientists in their Shroud project. The Academy is just north of several military complexes, including that of Los Alamos, remembered for its atomic bomb experiments. In this unlikely environment the Shroud of Turin would receive a scrutiny far removed from any in his history. Jackson and Jumper with their new associates in research under the aegis of the American Holy Shroud Guild invited some forty Shroud experts to a two-day conference, 23–24 March, at the Ramada Inn, an Albuquerque motel. As I commented at the opening session, 'Who would have ever dreamed that in 1977 in the American town of Albuquerque such an assortment of scientists, clergy, historians and writers would be brought together by a relic?' The conference included scientists from such diverse laboratories as the Jet Propulsion, Los Alamos, Air Force Weapons and Kodak. From Cambridge was Bishop John A. T. Robinson and from the Vatican, Msgr. Guilio Ricci. Specialities ranged from image enhancement and aerodynamics to archaeology and medicine. The 'intent' of the meeting was to serve two purposes: 1. To bring those attending up to date on what others were doing and 2. To serve as a workshop to prepare a specific research proposal to the authorities in Turin.

The recent Turin Commission report was very much in the minds of all and Father Rinaldi spoke of his disappointment in its findings. More specifically he quoted the International Sindonological Centre's critique asking why, though the chemical analysis of the stains on the Shroud did not isolate blood components, no effort was made to determine the true nature of the two basic colours on the cloth: the chiaroscuro responsible for the negative image and the darker colour of the 'blood stains'. Rinaldi also asked, 'Why hadn't there been a further studying of one of the most interesting findings of the Commission – the fact that the colouring substance of stained portions of threads removed from the cloth was limited only to the surface of the samples?' It was also wondered why the 1969 experts did not fully examine the reverse side of the cloth, even after they noted that the images did not penetrate to the other side when looking at a small unstitched section.

It was the attitude presented by the Turin establishment which irked the American Shroud enthusiasts most. Jesuit theologian from Loyola University, Francis Filas, who has spoken on television and radio throughout the United States, was adamant that it now be understood that '. . . the Shroud exists for the world and therefore is the strictly private possession of no person and no group, no matter what the legal title might be. Legal possession should be exercised for the purpose of protecting the Shroud from destruction, harm, ridicule and stupidity; not for any purpose of stifling research . . . Any aura of "secrecy" makes the Shroud a suspect subject for many.'

Three Anglican clergy were present at the conference which indicated an entirely new interest about which most Roman Catholic sindonologists were delighted. Bishop Robinson would head my list of those least likely to be interested in the relic but he had contacted Father Rinaldi and me about a 'renewed interest' he had taken; the first had come years ago when he read his mother's copy of Paul Vignon's opus. In an article for *Theology*, he would admit: 'Doubtless it will seem odd to many that I should be writing on this subject at all. What is the author of *Honest to God* up to, getting mixed up with a relic?' In the best tradition of Cambridge thinkers, Robinson has displayed a talent for seeking the truth from the least likely sources and for re-investigating cherished theological assumptions (witness his monumental *Redating the New Testament* which has given him the unexpected role of being the 'darling' of conservative churchmen!). As we have seen, Robinson's analysis of the Shroud in relationship to the Gospel accounts of the burial clothes has added some valuable insights. Jackson and Jumper became aware that the 3-D enhancement of the Shroud face make it even more apparent, than is the case with the normal photographs, that there is something holding back the intervening hair at the sides of the face and an unmistakable 'ridge' at the top of the head. Robinson sees this as the *sudarion*, a large handkerchief or neck-cloth – rather like triangular bandage folded or rolled diagonally as a jaw-band, functionally necessary before *rigor mortis* set in. This would explain the 'pinched' effect where the head narrows at the top and the 'white patch' at the crown of the head. Robinson was also willing to entertain the possibility being suggested that the image creation might be in the realm of a 'high intensity, short burst radiation of some sort'. Jumper had suggested a 'radiation occurring in a very short molecular burst of around three seconds' and Dr Jay Rogers, archaeologist and thermochemist from Los Alamos, spoke of an intense burst of light – what he called a 'flash photolysis'.

None of the speakers would go on record at this time saying that this was the reason for the nonpenetrating images but it was evident that this view had quietly come to be the most acceptable possibility. Eric Jumper recalled telling his grandmother about all the research concerning the Shroud with which he was involved and she retorted, 'What difference does it all make?'

Her grandson continued, 'Well, let's say that instead of being some sort of stain, the Shroud image is proved to be a scorch.'

Eric's young brother was fascinated by this line of approach, suggesting that 'perhaps scientists might be able to quantify the temperature of hell'.

Jumper and Rogers were the two speakers most ready to pursue the radiation possibility. The sepia colour of the Shroud body images and the fact that those images seemed not to have been affected by the 1532 fire fitted this conjecture. The 1532 fire was seen as 'the perfect thermal experiment'. On the basis of the known melting point of silver mixed, as it would have been, with some base metal, it was possible for Rogers to estimate that the temperature within the silver reliquary reached 200° to 300° before the relic was saved with water. A thermal gradient could be established and also an important guide for making judgments about how the image might have been created.

Rogers had indicated earlier that the computer studies tend to rule out altogether the chance that the image was painted: no linear strokes were indicated and there was no change of colour from dark to light tones. Rogers further explained:

If the image were painted, it had to be painted with a coloured material; otherwise, the artist could not observe the progress of his work. What coloured materials could have been used prior to the known history of the Shroud? Most would have been inorganic in an organic vehicle or water, e.g. ochre in oil or egg white. More unlikely would have been natural organic pigments or stains; however, many of them would have been plant or animal prophyrins, all of which contain characteristic metals. Purely organic materials can be rejected on obvious grounds. Purely inorganic pigments may not have been changed by the heating received at the time of the fire, but all organic colours should have suffered a change in proportion to the severity of the heating they received. The closer the organic vehicle or dye to a heated area, the greater should be its change of colour or density. No variation of colour with position is observed on the Shroud: shading is accomplished by variation of density, not colour. Tone remains constant with position. I believe that the obvious thermal gradient that existed at the time of the fire eliminates the possibility that any organic pigment, dye or stain was used, or that any common porphyrin pigment was used. The lack of observed capillary flow or absorption seems to eliminate most water-based inorganic systems from consideration . . . I also cannot see any evidence for migration of any of the image as a result of water percolation. If soluble pigments had been used, they would have moved. Many insoluble pigments would have produced soluble products as a result of the heat and reactive pyrolysis products of the cloth . . . The only conclusion that can be reached is that, if the image were painted, a stable, particulate inorganic pigment in a water base had to have been used . . . I believe the best way to test nondestructively for the presence or absence of inorganic pigments would be X-ray fluorescence, and I consider this analysis to be the most important nondestructive test that can be run during the 1978 viewing.

The damage caused by the 1532 fire was seen also as substantial proof against the vaporograph theory of Paul Vignon. The relic had been folded in a reliquary and so different parts of the Shroud would have been exposed to widely varying temperatures. Some of the Shroud cloth was darkened by the fire but interestingly enough these portions have the same colour tone and density as parts of the image at the greatest distance from the discoloured areas. Of this Rogers has stated, 'If large, complicated natural-product organic molecules were responsible for the image, they should have decomposed, changed colour or volatilised at different rates, depending on their distance from a high-temperature zone during the fire. There is no evidence for any variations at all.'

Further doubts about Vignon's hypothesis came to Eric Jumper with the discovery of the 'coin-like' images over the eyes: 'It is hard to imagine an organic stain mechanism acting to form not only images of the body but also of inert objects such as coins.' Another difficulty was the fact that the hair images followed the exact law of intensity versus distance as did the body image. Added to that is the fact that nowhere did the image intensity reach a plateau and remain at that intensity – nowhere on the body image was it saturated. The Turin Commission report had stated that the image was only a surface phenomenon as well, and it all seemed to point to some sort of 'radiation' process.

Rogers added his view that an image originally formed by thermal discolouration of the cloth would not change colour or density significantly by any additional heating as with the Chambery fire. Rogers noted that the computation of Jackson and Jumper in their cloth-body distance analysis had suggested rapid heating as the cause of the image.

Other scientists who have studied the subject have been more cautious than Rogers in pointing to this possibility. It does seem apparent, however, that if radiation is affirmed as the creation process it would have to be like flash photolysis – that is, extremely high-intensity light or heat for a very short time. There could be no other way without the linen being penetrated or destroyed.

It became apparent to all involved that with their tests, Jackson and Jumper with their associates had gone about as far as possible using photographs of the Shroud. What was next needed and hoped for was direct testing of the cloth itself. This was the discussion of the last day of the conference. The possibilities of tests and direct observations were so many and varied that there might be the opposite problem of what had happened with the Turin Commission, that of involving too many disciplines and too large a personnel. And, of course, it would all be conjecture for just how much would Turin be willing to accept or even be willing to consider? Radiocarbon dating was put at the top of the list and conference participant Walter McCrone was considered the person best suited to be in charge of this possibility. McCrone does not have facilities for such a test at his Chicago laboratory but he is in contact with the important C-14 centres which have greatly changed their methods from the original test developed in the 1940s by American physicist, Willard Libby.

Radiocarbon dating is based on some simple scientific truths. The nonmetallic element carbon is found in all living things in various forms and combinations. In all samples of carbon there are a few atoms (about one in a million million!) which are radioactive. The difference between the radioactive heavy carbon and ordinary carbon is the atomic weight; for the former 14 and for the latter 12. When plants and animals die, the intake of all forms of carbon ceases and the heavy carbon breaks down into nitrogen with the result that the radioactivity of the dead organism's tissues falls off in a regular manner. The organism's 'built-in clock' begins to run down and the carbon-14 atoms tick away the minutes and the years. On the average, in 5,568 years, only half of the original C-14 atoms are left; in another 5,568 years only half of those are left and so on until all the heavy carbon has decayed. Long before that time most plants and animals have decayed into dust. But some of these organisms have become fossilized or were changed into other substances like flax into linen or papyrus into paper. The ages of these remains can be calculated from the amount of radioactivity they still retain.

Libby's first experimental checks on the accuracy of radio-carbon dating were made on samples of already known age – heartwood from a giant sequoia tree and specimens of mummy cases and house beams. The results were good but never completely precise. They are given within a range of possible error of plus or minus 100 years; the precise date lying anywhere between. But the effects of Libby's test for museums and art galleries has been immeasurable. Radiocarbon dating has come to be the most important dating device of archaeologists. Dating some Egyptian specimens created some difficulties for a while but a valuable correction of errors was made with the Stuiver-Seuss method in the 1960s using the infallible bristlecone pine tree-ring chronology.

The chief disadvantage to the original Libby test for many art objects and artifacts was the fact that it required 20–25 gram samples. Few art pieces could afford that generous a piece to be destroyed. This has radically altered in this decade as the following chart provided by Walter McCrone indicates:[68]

Date	Sample weight	Sample area
1950	40 gm	40 x 40 cm
1970	20 gm	30 x 30 cm
1971	5 gm	14 x 14 cm
1973	2.5 gm	10 x 10 cm
1974	600 mg	5 x 5 cm
1977	60 mg	1.6 x 1.6 cm

In North America three separate groups of experimenters, working independently of one another have shown almost simultaneously that carbon dating with an accelerator (used as a mass spectrometer to separate C-14 from other carbon isotopes) is now feasible: Lawrence Berkeley Laboratory in California, the University of Rochester with University of Toronto, Simon Fraser and McMaster Universities. The latter two groups use a van de Graff particle accelerator: Lawrence Berkeley employs a cyclotron. The new methods are able to measure C-14 directly rather than the rate of decay of the C-14 content of a sample as by the Libby method. The sample to be tested is placed in the accelerator where the carbon 14 and carbon 12 are separated; by comparing the ratio of the two types of carbon the age of the studied sample can be calculated. This method of direct measurement will require one-hundredth of the material previously needed which means that the two samples removed for Professor

Raes would be sufficient enough to be sub-divided giving the possibility of several tests instead of one.

Walter McCrone's laboratory in Chicago has an extensive collection of microanalytical tools which could determine every conceivable element comprising the linen samples. The ion microprobe (of which there are only about twenty in the world – all in the United States) is a particularly valuable instrument considering that the stains of the Shroud are visible only one one side of the individual fibres. The ion microprobe can identify all 104 elements in the periodic table and the amount of each element present in a particular sample. Its sensitivity exceeds that of the electron microprobe by a factor of more than a thousand.

We know, of course, the chemical composition of human flesh and blood as well as the possible chemicals and pigments used to create any painting or artifact. Once we know what elements are to be found with the Shroud's stains and the linen fabric and in what quantities and in what distribution they are to be found, it should be possible to determine much about how the images were formed. Dr McCrone has said about the ion microprobe:

> It detects, on one tiny spot on one of my scalp hairs, for example, more than thirty trace elements attesting to the fact that such a hair can only have come from my head, the calcium level ensures good cell membrane equilibria, the iron level that I am not anaemic, the potassium level that my hyperactivity is under reasonably good control, the zinc that I need not fear schizophrenia and the lithium is protection against manic depressive behaviour. Finally, the vanadium and chromium levels announce that I am 60 + 2–3 years.

There is another ultra-microanalytical tool capable of identifying organic and inorganic molecules – micro Raman spectroscopy. This instrument became available commercially only in March 1977 and yields information which is equivalent to infrared absorption, but on samples nearly one million times smaller. Dr Stuart Fleming when he was at Oxford

University's Research Laboratory for Archaeology gave valuable advice on test possibilities for me to pass on to the Turin authorities and strongly recommended this method: 'If the normal cellulose structure of the Shroud's linen incorporates any strange dyestuff, any ammonia-based molecular configuration, any by-product of cellulose produced by heat . . . or any elements from spices like aloes, Raman spectroscopy should find it. It is probably the right tool to use now in a fresh search for blood components (particularly chemically-stable porphyrins), as its sensitivity must be close to a thousand times greater than the methods used by Frache in 1973.'

Analytical chemical techniques such as those used by McCrone have had some important decision making results in the art world. In 1970, the Uffizi Gallery in Florence recatalogued a portrait of Pope Julius II as being 'after Raphael' (by a student or in the manner of the artist). London's National Gallery possessed another version of the portrait and it was thought by the trustees that their painting should be analysed in the light of the Uffizi's decision. Indicated in tests was the presence of walnut oil in the medium employed by the painter and art historians knew that Raphael was one of the few painters of his time to favour the unique oil. This evidence with X-ray photographs which had revealed changes and experiments in Raphael's usual manner convinced the art world that the original painting was the one in the National Gallery.

X-ray photography was considered in New Mexico to be an important aspect of the Shroud's future testing. This technique is simple and non-destructive and is able to find out methods used to create an art object or historical artifact. It depends upon the fact that as X-rays pass through an object, they are absorbed in varying degrees, depending upon the kinds of material incorporated in the object. X-ray photographs have clearly revealed outlines of underpaintings which sometimes makes it apparent that a forger has been at work or, as in the case of Raphael's 'Pope Julius II', techniques of experimentation by the artist himself.

As previously stated, Dr Ray Rogers had stated at the Albuquerque conference that he considered X-ray fluorescence to be the most important nondestructive test which could be performed with the Shroud. It would be able to detect the presence of iron in the 'blood stain' areas of the image. Indeed, its use can indicate characteristically high concentrations of any trace elements. X-ray fluorescence spectroscopy depends on the fact that if an object is bombarded with a primary beam of X-rays, a beam of secondary X-rays (the fluorescence) will be emitted. This fluorescence will be determined by the elements present in the sample object. By comparing the sample's fluorescence with standards based on emissions from known samples, the scientist can tell what elements are present and their approximate concentration. In the case of the Shroud, particular attention would be paid not only to iron but also phosphorous indicating a blood possibility as well; chlorine for sweat, silver for the burning reliquary casket in Chambery; and high atomic number metals which might display those pigments of which Rogers spoke in respect to a painting possibility. This test received a top priority on the possible agenda.

Bumblebees can see light in both visible and ultraviolet wave-lengths. UV photographs can vividly display the nectar area of flowers to which bees are attracted and has also been employed as a detection tool by art museums to display recent alterations made with paintings and other art objects. Unlike X-ray photography, UV does not 'uncover' a fake but will cause retouchings such as those suggested by Professor Curto to fluoresce. Some scientists at the New Mexico meeting indicated that UV might give clues as to the nature of the 'blood stains' on the Shroud.

Another form of radiation, infrared (at the red end of the visible spectrum which relates possibly to the general colour 'make-up' of the Shroud) might indicate a heretofore unexplained image. Infrared sensors can measure temperature differences to picture the heat radiating from a man's face or escaping from a house in winter. These images are thermographs, heat pictures, and are unique '. . . because the minute differences in contrast from point to point that create an (infrared) image are caused by changes in temperature rather than changes in reflection, as in the case of conventional photography' according to Joseph Accetta, a specialist in the field at the Air Force Weapons Laboratory. Accetta wanted to see an infrared analysis of the Shroud, pointing out that '. . . substances can sometimes be identified by measuring the relative amounts of radiation present in a series of narrow energy regions in the infrared. This technique forms a characteristic spectrum that is sometimes unique to a specific material or substance. By measuring this 'signature' we hope to identify one or more substances that might be responsible for the image.'

Infrared rays penetrating darkened illegible parts of the Dead Sea Scrolls made it possible to read the hidden letters. Juan de Flandes' charcoal underdrawing of the Annunciation with his distinctive shading technique were revealed by infrared, making it possible for the National Gallery in London to verify the work as by the sixteenth century Flemish artist.

When Dr Donald Lynn of The University of California's Jet Propulsion Laboratory subjected Judica-Cordiglia's colour photographs (which to the human eye seem two basic colours – the faint sepia of the body image and the burn marks plus the darker brown of the blood-stains) to colour-scanning in his laboratory in Pasadena, California, the results indicated that there is really only one colour in all the aspects of the Shroud. All recorded the same intensity which has led some to conclude yet again that the creation process of the Shroud is a type of 'scorch'. This information pointed to the need for photographs taken especially for scientific analysis. The weave pattern of the linen, for example, could be eliminated by special filtering processes. New photographs tailored to be translated into numbers for further computer analysis are needed. One square inch of film would be represented by a million separate points, each of which would describe the relative darkness and light at each point. The possibilities of this type of investigation are 'essentially infinite' according to Lynn. Textural differences at any point on the cloth and the relative darkness of each bloodstain would be accurately measured.

Lynn's laboratory worked on the photographs beamed back from the Viking Mission to Mars and his analysis of Shroud photographs has already revealed some interesting information:

1. The water marks and numerous small intense features on the body have abrupt edges, whereas the large burn marks have smoothly decaying edges. This suggests a different mechanism of formation for the two types of features.
2. The short, linear marks with small spots along them, which appear on the back of the figure, could be attributed to scourge marks. These marks seem to be separable into two different, predominately diagonal directions (indicating possibly that two men carried out the flogging or one man used two different positions).
3. The image of the facial region is composed of a wide range of spatial frequences that are oriented in a random fashion. This indicates that the feature-generating mechanism was probably directionless (a characteristic that would not be consistent with hand application thus providing additional evidence that the image was not painted).

There was no doubt that there were enough indications at the New Mexico conference that new expert tests were needed and it was fairly evident as to which might prove most useful. The comprehensive 'package' of proposals set forth would mean that the Shroud would be examined with electro-magnetic radiation over a wide range of wave lengths: infrared, ultraviolet and X-ray. Like a horse with blinkers, man sees only a narrow band of electro-magnetic spectrum that spans the radiant energy common to all things. Those 'blinkers' are being removed by a variety of sophisticated techniques. Such a range of wavelengths would present a wealth of information which could be correlated into an extensive assessment of the Shroud's make-up and image creation. Added to this would be microanalysis and carbon-dating. Few artifacts or art objects have ever faced such a barrage of high-powered testing. This indicates both the complexities of the mystery of the Shroud and the seriousness with which it has come to be considered in the 1970s.

CHAPTER 7

HOW WAS THE SHROUD BROUGHT TO THE TESTS IN 1978?

The success of the New Mexico conference with its important analysis of Turin's testing and its own impressive test proposals was a tribute to the effectiveness of the American Holy Shroud Guild. The guild has grown from being the efforts of a few dedicated sindonologists at its founding in 1951 to encompassing a large number of experts from a variety of special fields. Interest in the Turin Shroud in Britain has been much more scattered and less organised compared to the American effort. For many years, individuals such as Group Captain Leonard Cheshire, Dr David Willis and Vera Barclay acted as sources of information on the Shroud in Great Britain. Cheshire's Mission for the Relief of Suffering handled requests for photographs and answered the various queries concerning the relic. Following the death of David Willis, who had taken considerable responsibility upon himself, Cheshire and others felt that an independent society should be formed to continue his and other independent efforts. The initiating group took on an 'ecumenical flavour' early with the involvement of Bishop Robinson and myself. Ian Wilson's historical research and Robinson's New Testament expertise gave the group an early academic tone. The idea for a symposium on the various aspects of investigation on the Shroud was thought to be a good way to inaugurate the new group, the British Society for the Turin Shroud. Continuing its ecumenical inception, the symposium was held at the Anglican Institute of Christian Studies, 16–17 September 1977.

Unlike the New Mexico conference, the London symposium was open to subscribers and those who attended were from surprisingly diverse backgrounds: Muslim, Jewish, Methodist, Greek Orthodox, and Anglican as well as the expected large number of Roman Catholics and many with no religious persuasion. *The Times* 'Diary' of early August stated, 'Now the Shroud of Mystery Reaches London' and the diarist continued '. . . I cannot resist the temptation to see the "all star" cast in action . . .' 'All star' it was with almost every important speaker, writer or thinker on the subject present: Jackson and Jumper with their colleagues, Rinaldi, Otterbein and McCrone from the United States; Msgr. Ricci and Don Coero-Borga from Italy, Max Frei from Zurich and all the English sindonologists. The 'Diary' article started an interest on the part of the media which was to reach *blitzkrieg* proportions the day the symposium began. More than one hundred participants and newsmen pressed into a hall anticipating little more than fifty.

A surprise was the interest Turin took in the event. *La Stampa*, the Turin-based newspaper, and *RAI*, the Italian television company, sent a group of personnel to cover the proceedings. *La Stampa* announced with one head-line, 'London Proposes: the Shroud Should Undergo New Tests'. They were especially fascinated by the non-Roman Catholic interest expressed and the fact that the meeting was occurring in Britain, '. . . undoubtedly an exceptional event in a country which, since its separation from the Papacy, has always shown a great deal of scepticism – if not downright hostility towards similar forms of cult'.

The ground had been prepared for what was to follow. Jumper, Jackson, Rinaldi and Otterbein left London the day following the symposium to present the 'New Mexico proposals' to a new commission in Turin set up under the aegis of the International Centre for Sindonology.

The proposals were now refined to suggest:

1. Carbon dating.
2. More pollen analysis.

3. Ion microprobe analysis.
4. Radiographic and X-ray fluorescent examination, micro-photography, infrared and ultraviolet study; new colour photography and a complete coverage with black and white photographs in whole and sections of the Shroud.
5. Extensive examination of the reverse of the relic done with a flexible optical instrument so as not to have to unstitch the backing cloth from the Shroud.

The initial reaction was most encouraging – it was apparent the Turin commission was impressed with what was being proposed. The American team had done its 'homework' and towards the end of the last session of talks, Don Pietro Caramello, who had been the president of the 1969–73 commission, suggested that letters with the recommendations should be sent to the new Archbishop and King Umberto.

Cardinal Pellegrino's resignation for reasons of health had been accepted by Pope Paul by this time and his newly named successor, Anastasio Ballestrero, had not assumed his new role when these talks took place. Ballestrero's first feeling as to what should be done in 1978 to mark the four hundredth anniversary of the Shroud's being in Turin was to seek a wide consensus in Turin of clergy and laity by circulating a questionnaire through ecclesiastical channels. When Father Rinaldi and I saw him before Christmas 1977, we both remarked how much he looked like Pope John XXIII. Ballestrero is a member of the Carmelite order and was well liked by the clergy of Bari where he had served as bishop. He was surprised that there was so much Anglican interest in the Shroud and listened attentively to the proposals for the Shroud's further study. One sensed a spiritual concern for the relic and he left no doubt that he favoured an exposition far removed from any commercialism which would make an adverse impression upon Turin's Communist government and would be totally out of keeping with his feelings for the relic. Ballestrero's new office automatically carried a cardinalate but he remained without the 'red hat' when Paul VI died. His name was mentioned as Paul's successor despite this fact; *Time* magazine (21 August 1978) described him as 'Perhaps the most attractive Italian of all (candidates) . . .' Peter Nichols in *The Times* (8 August) gave the reasons: 'The chances of the Archbishop of Turin . . . were running high, explicitly because he is a member of a religious order with little interest in political affairs and credited with a much more spiritual view of his duties than is the case with many Italian bishops. At the same time he had the qualities which make Italians useful at the Vatican.'

King Umberto had been aware of Walter McCrone's proposed C-14 test programme for at least two years when I visited him at his villa in Portugal in July 1977 and he reiterated at that time his interest in allowing the carbon dating by 'competent authorities'. McCrone's proposal was now three-fold:

1. The carbon dating test done by two different laboratories using the available samples plus similar ancient linen samples from other objects.
2. Microanalysis of body fluid stains and images of individual fibres using electron, ion and possibly laser microprobes plus Raman spectroscopy (all executed before the carbon dating of the samples).
3. Analysis of dust particles from the samples which would be part of the cleaning operation prior to the carbon test.

This final point offered some fascinating possibilities. 'Dust' collected by a 'micro-vacuum cleaner' would include years of biological and mineral substances. These particles would not only include pollen which could be studied by Dr Frei but minerals characteristic of the localities through which the Shroud has passed and could be analysed by the powerful microprobes in McCrone's laboratory. The sampling would also have a beneficial side-effect – removing hard abrasive particles of sand and limestone which now abrade the linen fibres whenever the Shroud is moved.

A week after I had seen King Umberto, Monsignor Giulio Ricci and his secretary, Mary Elizabeth Patrizzi, visited him.

Msgr. Ricci, archivist at the Vatican for the Congregation of Bishops, has had a long-time interest in the Shroud. He probably knows more about each individual marking on the relic than any other person and his Roman Centre for Sindonology is so efficiently run that it has given the impression to tourists of being the official Italian centre on the subject. There can be no doubt that Ricci and Patrizzi were given the impression at the New Mexico conference that they should pursue 'diplomatic overtures', for the possible carbon test and that they did. On 21 September, following the meeting in Turin, the two with Dr McCrone met King Umberto in Geneva to discuss the project. A phone call to Msgr. Caramello in Turin ascertained that the 'Raes samples' were still in the Cathedral sacristy safe and Miss Patrizzi indicated that the King had authorised their release for testing. Caramello apparently wanted more than a phone call as assurance of the King's desire and nothing came of this manoeuvre.

It had always been felt important that 'Shroud related samples' be tested before the Turin Shroud portions themselves and Msgr. Ricci was able to obtain portions of the Spanish relic, *El Sagrado Rostro* or *El Santo Sudario* as it is alternately called from the ancient Oviedo Cathedral. This image is little known outside Spain and was reportedly brought to Oviedo in the ninth century, and is now enshrined in a simple wooden frame covered with silver plate of the seventeenth century. It is a stained piece of linen measuring 83cm. by $52\frac{1}{2}$ cm. with a close knit weaving. According to one priest who has studied the article, Father Bernardo Salazar, 'When you watch (the stains) for the first time you get the same impression that you get from the sight of the Holy Shroud of Turin . . . the stains look like being of watery blood, oil, aloes and balsam and keep diminishing in intensity from the centre of the linen until they finally fade away. The location of these two big central stains seems to form a kind of a square of about 30cm. each side . . . it could be thought that the sacred linen was applied to the face of the Lord when he was laid in a horizontal position, because they give you the impression of having been on the cheeks, and the temple cavities of the corpse of Jesus when he was already wrapped in the Holy Shroud . . .'[69] Other interpreters assumed that the cloth was folded and used as a kind of pillow for the head of Jesus.

The measurements could easily fit the idea of the *sudarion* as a jaw-band passing crossways over the head, round the face and under the chin, holding the mouth shut before *rigor mortis* set in. Father Salazar's remark concerning contact with the temple areas also makes this an interesting speculation as to the relic's identity.

Walter McCrone prepared two samples of the Oviedo linen for testing as would be the case for the hoped-for Shroud material. The samples were first ultrasonerated in a filter funnel to remove all dust particles which was collected on a membrane filter for microscopical and microprobe analysis. Next was the weighing of the sample material from which a portion was cut and dissolved in freshly prepared aqueous cuprous ammonium hydroxide. The cellulose was then precipitated by adding hydrochloric acid. After repeated washing and final drying the 'regenerated cellulose' was a thin translucent film which could be easily weighed preparatory to oxidation to carbon dioxide. Pure carbon dioxide of the material could be quickly carbon-dated by the improved methods of several North American laboratories. The carbon dioxide of the Oviedo relic was placed in U-tubes which were specially fitted with connections compatible with the sampling system on the cyclotron used by the Lawrence Berkeley Laboratory in California which was always favoured by McCrone as one of the laboratories to be considered for the Shroud dating test.

Seven fibres had been individually isolated for ion microprobe study and some of these showed the dark stains described by Father Salazar. McCrone stated he was able to find the following elements 'associated with the stains': calcium, sodium, magnesium, aluminum, silicon, potassium, titanium, manganese, iron, nickel, cobalt, copper, zinc and arsenic. The analysis of dust particles which have been identified included short linen and silk fibres, cotton, starch, quartz, limestone, feldspars, red and yellow pigments, iron oxide, flash (trash burning), coal, epithelial cells, pollens and spores. No conclusions were drawn from that information at that time.

The Lawrence Berkeley laboratory felt that its accelerator needed some improvements and the carbon dating of the Oviedo samples was postponed. Another set-back to having the Shroud samples carbon-dated was the interpretation given to the results of an electron scanning of a thread taken from the Shroud by Princess Clotilde, Napoleon III's wife, when the relic's lining was repaired by her in 1868. This thread under analysis revealed traces of many sorts. The amount of what seemed to some as 'contaminating elements' was alarming, giving rise to fears that a carbon test might be greatly affected. Professor Luigi Baima Bollone was unable to arrive at any definitive conclusion with his scanning of the thread because the contaminating agents were present in such great quantities. Other experts stressed the importance of the 'cleaning process' which would precede the carbon test would remove the contamination. This experiment, however, was enough to add weight to the general uneasy feeling many in Turin had concerning what the C-14 test might disclose.

On 20 January 1978, the new Archbishop of Turin, with the permission of the Pope and King Umberto, announced that the longest exposition of the Shroud to be held in modern times and the first public one since 1933, would be from 27 August to 8 October. During the last two days of the public showing an International Congress of Sindonology would occur, the first since 1950. Monsignor Cottino was to be in charge of the exposition and Don Coero Borga's office would organise the congress.

There had been no further word about the fate of the proposed tests until the finalised recommendations for the Archbishop's approval were issued on 24 April 1978. That he would accept was a foregone conclusion but it was the absence of a carbon dating test proposal which attracted the most attention. The report stated that '. . . since we (the members of the recommending commission) do not have a consensus among the experts on the one-hundred-per-cent efficacy of this test in the specific case of the Shroud' it was postponed 'for the present'. It was unfortunate that the recommendation suggesting further pollen analysis which followed the remarks on C-14 testing, was seen as giving 'very positive results to the age and history of the Shroud' hinting that this test could be seen as a satisfactory substitution. This view had been expressed before in Turin and indicated the continuing misunderstanding of what pollen analysis could indicate. All the other tests proposed by Jackson and Jumper's team were recommended.

When Father Rinaldi released the report to me he wrote, 'I know the first paragraph must come as a disappointment to you. But that is the way it is. I have told the members of the Scientific Commission to be prepared for a first-class battle on the Carbon-14 test during the Congress.' What worried some of us the most was the simple fact that the Congress came at the end of the exposition and if new tiny samples were needed to augment those already removed – as had been suggested by some in Turin and elsewhere, the time for removal would have to be the proposed day of testing which was 9 October. After that the relic would be returned to its reliquary not to be reopened for who knows how many years. *The Times* of 9 May released the proposal information on its front page under the heading, 'Carbon 14 Test Rejected for Shroud'. I was listed as the source of the information and found myself again in the middle of the arguments for carbon dating.

Fortunately I was able to report this time that there was a laboratory which was able to perform the new carbon test – the Nuclear Structure Research Laboratory at the University of Rochester in New York state. Rochester and Lawrence Berkeley laboratory in California had been in a healthy competitive race to perfect the machinery of their carbon dating facilities. In the early part of the summer of 1978 Lawrence Berkeley was trying to eliminate the interference of extraneous carbon-14 in the cyclotron chamber of their laboratory. This was created by the separate nuclear experiments for which the accelerator was designed to perform. Richard Muller of Lawrence Berkely felt that this interference could not be removed without building a completely new source and this his laboratory set out to do. This had caused the laboratory to indefinitely postpone carbon testing the Oviedo samples and this information caused some in Turin to question the possibility of the test by any laboratory at an early date. The Archbishop of Turin expressed his worry at the seemingly contradictory statements about carbon dating to Father Rinaldi. There seemed to be little doubt that he was beginning to realise the importance of the test but it was equally apparent that those who could perform the test would be required to do a good job of convincing Turin.

Dr Harry Gove's laboratory at Rochester did not seem to have Lawrence Berkeley's problem when I visited it in June 1978. Canadian television had taken an interest in the possibility of Rochester being able to perform the test and they were especially interested because the project was linked with the nearby University of Toronto. Dr Gove and I were interviewed by them during a session of accuracy level tests Rochester was performing. My first contact with Harry Gove had come from reading a *Time* magazine article about the success his team of researchers was having in directly measuring carbon-14 with extremely small sample material. Gove is an impressive figure – easily irritated but highly competent in his field. The research laboratory at Rochester is pretty much his creation and he is enthusiastic about its record and potentiality. The principal instrument of his laboratory is the Model MP Tandem van de Graaf accelerator, affectionately known as 'the Emperor' and it is housed in a massive orange steel pressure tank eighty feet long.

Gove explains the difference between his method and the older carbon test in this manner: 'In the past, scientists have determined the age of objects by measuring their carbon-14 radioactivity. This is like waiting for a clock to tick in order to determine its existence. Our method does not require us to wait for the radioactive ticks of carbon-14, but measures the amount directly . . . You could say we're detecting the clock rather than its ticks.' By the time the Shroud was being publicly exhibited in Turin, Gove was able to present a proposal for dating the Shroud which I delivered to Turin for the Congress's proceedings. Using Professor Raes' useful measurements of his samples it was estimated that 1cm. length of warp thread would produce 0.032mg. of carbon and the same length of the coarser weft thread would give 0.10mg. of carbon. Carbon constitutes one fifth of the weight of linen. Three 20cm. long weft threads and two or three 63cm. length warp threads would be ideal samples. If one portion of sample were seen as preferable, measurement of a 10mm. square would be sufficient. These were fairly conservative estimates but again proved that Raes' samples could be used for several tests. Dr Gove indicated that the test would take only a few hours and there was the possibility of a +1% accuracy level which corresponds to an age uncertainty of ±80 years.

The thoroughness of the sample cleaning process outlined by Dr Gove in his proposal seemed to rule out of order the concern expressed in Turin over the effects of contamination. In this process, the samples would be boiled for about sixteen hours in a 10% hydrochloric acid solution. Then they would be washed in distilled water and boiled again for another sixteen hours in concentrated hydrochloric acid followed by another washing. Next, the samples would be treated in sodium hydroxide at a temperature of 85°C for half an hour and again washed in distilled water. Finally, the samples would be boiled in 10% hydrochloric acid for two hours and rinsed in distilled water and then they would be dried. Gove suggested that veteran carbon dating expert, Meyer Rubin, of the United States Geological Survey, should be the overseer of this procedure which would mean the conversion of the cleansed samples into amorphous carbon. After the final cleaning, the samples would be placed in a small oven through which nitrogen gas is allowed to gently flow. The oven would be heated to a temperature of 300°C for a few hours. At the end of this process only carbon would remain – all the other chemical constituents of the cloth would be removed. Very little, if any, of the original carbon in the samples would be lost.

When I first approached Harry Gove about the possibility of dating the Shroud he had some reservations: '. . . it is possible to argue that important symbols of this kind that appeal to fundamental human beliefs and needs perhaps should not be subjected to scientific tests,' he wrote in an early communication. But he was becoming convinced with other scientists that there was only one test which could answer the most important question about the Shroud – how old is it?

Preparations for the other tests were moving along smoothly by the time the 'United States Conference of Research on the Shroud of Turin' (as Jackson and Jumper's group was now being called) met in Lebanon, Connecticut on 2–3 September. This was to be a final analysis of the test situation plus a complete simulation of the various tests. Turin had agreed to a twenty-four hour test period on 9 October so as Eric Jumper stated, 'These tests will have to go off with the same efficiency as a moon shot. We could get enough data in twenty-four hours of testing to keep us busy for thirty years after the information has been reduced by computer.' It was becoming apparent that because a number of scientists would be working on different tests at the same time or in close succession that the most important planning was the 'choreography' of what would transpire. Priority and scheduling was carefully planned in Connecticut. Thought was given to every detail: What electrical outlets and current would be available? What equipment would be available there? How much would have to be shipped over? The first problem was easily checked out with Father Rinaldi. It was decided to bring over 'everything but the dark room!' Material not needed for future use would be given to educational and charitable institutions in Turin. The concern which had been expressed at the September meeting in Turin over the amount of radiation which would be produced by the tests was laid to rest by Joseph Accetta's estimations that '. . . there is no way that the amount of radiation that we are going to produce . . . the amount of molecular disruption couldn't be more than one part in 10^7 which is hardly enough to cause any kind of damage to the image at all'.

The test costs were being estimated at between $120,000 to $150,000 and were being covered by a variety of private sources through the Holy Shroud Guild. Much of the X-ray radiographic, infrared, X-ray fluorescence, photographic and spectroscopic equipment was being loaned to the group of twenty-five who would be involved. Kodak had volunteered X-ray film for the fluorescence and radiographic tests. One of the costliest articles was the construction of a giant frame with soft magnets to hold the Shroud during the tests. A data link with the Los Alamos computers via satellite for immediate feedback on experimental progress was contemplated. The wives of several of the testers were going to be employed as 'logistic support technicians' to save further manpower costs.

Suggestions for some supporting tests were also made:

1. Photomicrographs to be made during testing to determine the mechanical properties of the Shroud on a microscopic scale (Is the cloth more or less pliable in the areas of the stains?).

2. Off-normal photography on a microscopic scale should be made in order to determine possible surface orientations of the image on individual threads.

3. An inspection of the reverse side of the Shroud between the backing cloth and the linen relic should be made especially at the locations of the blood spots.

4. John Jackson suggested that tape samples be taken from the image itself. This would mean the removal of tiny trace amounts of the image for exact and definitive testing later and would cause no harm to the image. These surface samples would include minute fibres and globules which could be examined with a process known as ESCA (electron spectroscopy for chemical analysis). This was not unlike what Dr

McCrone had originally planned to do at his laboratory in Chicago. The tape used would have to be one which didn't have any chemical functional group on it. The chemists at the meeting were excited about the possible wealth of chemical information which could be obtained from this procedure.

Of those preparing the October tests, Ray Rogers was the one who talked the most about the possible implications of what was being planned. He explained how his thinking had progressed from the time of the New Mexico conference, 'What I have done was go ahead with the list of hypotheses that I put in the 1977 proceedings and looked at the facts I thought were sort of uncontrovertible. Here I listed facts . . . colour on one side only, no capillary flow of the coloured medium, no diffusion into the fibres of the Shroud . . . The colour is discontinuous on the fibre bundles . . .'

After the New Mexico meeting, Rogers had made a heat flow calculation on the Shroud as it would have been folded up at the time of the 1532 fire and then predicted thermal gradients across the cloth and looked at what kinds of reaction rates would have been expected in the cloth and in any kind of material which might have been used to paint the image. Rogers felt that 'It is a very steep gradient and this should have made a tremendous effect on anything that was there either as a natural pigment, or a large natural organic molecule, or any of the materials to paint with.' He further speculated that after the series of experiments he made, '. . . the probability of having a natural iron pigment that was available at the time of say 1300 (or something like that) is zilch . . . because you can see a blackening of iron pigments . . .' All other pigments as well would have been affected by the powerful reducing agents in the anaerobic atmosphere which occurred in the closed-up chest of the 1532 fire with the cloth smouldering inside. There would have been a tremendous reaction on the linen and its images.

Rogers indicated other implications of his analysis: 'There was no movement of the colour, no colour change, and no movement of the blood stains with the water that was poured on to put the fire out . . . There was no impedance to the flow of the water and I think this is tremendously important, too, because if any vehicle or medium had been used as the painting system . . . the water flow through it would have been impeded by the medium that was absorbed in the fibres and the medulla of these fibres. There was impedance to the water flow of the image for the water marks are symmetrical.'

Rogers stated further that he felt the image and blood marks were fluorescent. He wasn't sure at what wavelength the illuminating light was and that would be important to pursue in October but he could say, 'There's one way that I've been able to find so far of making linen fluorescent in that colour, and that's only by scorching. The scorches on the Shroud are fluorescent, the image is fluorescent, the blood marks are fluorescent, and that's the only way I can get there.' The image is fluorescent but all the pigment or vehicle possibilities that could be considered are not fluorescent.

Rogers also discussed the fact that the blood spots not only fluoresce and are insoluble but they are not saturated. 'Every one of those blood spots that I have been able to look at microscopically in photographs do not saturate the cloth. You can still see uncoloured threads in the zone of the blood spots. Blood doesn't fluoresce. There is only one way that it fluoresces naturally and that's in a disease called porphyra . . . My bets are that it is a metaporphyrin that causes the fluorescence in the porphyria of blood and that is not one of the world's most stable compounds either to heat or formaldehyde. I think that it would be quenched of fluorescence by the heating, water, etc.'

It was also noted that in a real sense, the most extraordinary 'experiments' had already occurred with the Shroud in its past. The October tests would have to continue to take the implications of these episodes into consideration. As Rogers put it, 'Who would let us now put (the Shroud) through a fire and dump water on it, wash it, dip it in hot oil, or anything of the like which has already been done to it.'

Near the time of the Congress, Rogers and others again stressed the importance of investigating the back side of the cloth behind the blood spots to see whether it could be demonstrated that 'the back side of the blood spots are indeed fluorescent or show a higher density without saturation . . . If we can, I think part of the game is over'. Donald Lynn of the Jet Propulsion Laboratory stressed the importance of some of Rogers' findings:

> Ray is saying that if the fibres were heated (perhaps with a short burst of intense radiation) they curl up and create discontinuous spots. He has looked at magnified pictures and, in fact, the images are discontinuous. They are not lines, they are a series of spots. So what we have is a mechanism that does support the range information if it were a scorch (or this sort of thing) and would cause such curling up which would definitely point to a scorch. This is not saying how the radiation got there. But that at least gets an image on the cloth, an image which fits the criteria that there is range in it and the other things we see, especially the high resolution suggesting highly directional source.

On 24 September it was announced that two Italian electronic experts, Giovanni Tamburelli and Giovanni Garbotto of the University of Turin, were claiming a confirmation of the computerised images of the Shroud done by Jackson and Jumper in 1976. The Italians' computerised photographs strongly resembled the earlier ones by the Americans. This was a good boost to the American team as they finalised their test plans. John Jackson had wisely sought outside advice and suggestions from scientists in Britain and Europe. The British Society for the Turin Shroud was able to give scientific support not only to the carbon dating proposal but also in other directions. Dr Allan Mills of the University of Leicester suggested electron spin resonance as a useful tool in research on the Shroud since some of the hypotheses for the origin of the Shroud had involved brief exposure of the linen to intense heat or radiation – 'flash pyrolysis'. As Mills stressed, 'If scorching is indeed involved then we might expect this to give rise to a positive and characteristic ESR signal . . . and it might also be possible to investigate the nature of the "blood stains", for such an origin should leave a residue containing iron-bearing pigments derived from haemoglobin.' Experiments relevant to this suggestion indicated that they seemed to be on the right track. The chief problem, however, was the number of samples that Mills' laboratory desired: 'fragments or threads totalling about one square centimetre in area from 1/ an unmarked portion (for control purposes), 2/ an area damaged by the fire, 3/ an image-bearing portion and 4/ a bloodstain portion.'

A more exotic proposal came from Gregory Winter of the Medical Research Laboratory of Molecular Biology at Cambridge. Winter like others is interested in identifying the precise nature of the image and 'blood stains'. According to his outlined proposal, the organic molecules still residing on the cloth could prove to be the key to establishing the nature of the stains. 'For example,' writes Winter, 'the identification of the stable porphyrin groups of the haemoglobin molecule in the blood stains would confirm their authenticity.' Like others we have noted, Winter points out that the issue is complicated by the possible chemical changes elicited by pyrolysis products during the 1532 fire. 'It may, therefore, prove necessary to distinguish between porphyrin derivatives.' Winter suggests field desorption mass spectrometry which gives well defined ion peaks on about 1mg. of purified porphyrin and different porphyrins can be readily distinguished. 'Blood normally contains around 5mg. porphyrin per microlitre. One microlitre corresponds to about one hundredth of a drop of blood and so the expected levels of porphyrins lie well within the sensitivity of the technique.' Winter points out that the same tiny sample used for this test could easily be used again for carbon dating which he strongly favours.

There was another element to Winter's proposed test which he has downplayed because of the possible implications. 'The long term possibility concerns rescuing and cloning residual DNA in the cloth. Red blood cells do not have nuclei and do not contain the genetic material, DNA. However, white cells are generally nucleated and comprise ~1%

of the volume of the blood. These cells would contain most of the genetic information of the individual concerned. Thus, copies of portions of Christ's genes could become available to the Roman Catholic Church for whatever purposes it considers appropriate.' Winter admits this is speculative but the sensitivity in cloning technology is improving rapidly and what he has suggested may not seem so outrageous in the future.

The nearer the time approached for the October Congress, the more suggestions were forthcoming for analysing the Shroud. Newspapers in the United States carried reports of individual scientists suggesting the application of laser testing and holograph photography. The latter was being pushed by New York holographer, Jerry Goldblatt, who has formulated a 'holographic-laser' theory to account for the mystery of the Shroud. He believes the image contains two pictures: the one discernible to the naked eye which functions as a photographic negative and a second that is a three-dimensional hologram impressed in the cloth. Goldblatt has explained his view in this manner, 'I believe both images were caused simultaneously when laser light revived the lifeless body in the shroud, triggering off a thermonuclear explosion that lasted for a millisecond of time. The body was transformed molecularly, which enabled it to pass through the shroud, while radiant heat scorched the negative image onto the cloth in a precise and controlled manner for only a millisecond, thus not damaging the fibre.' Goldblatt has pointed out that recent scientific experiments show that it is theoretically possible to make molecules of the human body 'lase' – to emit powerful, concentrated light – if the body's molecules are stimulated by an external force of the same frequency.

There was hardly any inquiry from the most exacting new scientific procedure to the most questionable psychic possibility which had not had something to add as the Shroud was being removed for its exposition in late August. An enthusiast of sacred geometry wrote to the *Sunday Times* about a 'small experiment' which he had made with the Shroud's dimensions. These were converted into Royal

Egyptian cubits, obtaining 17.29 sq. cubits. He stated, 'In sacred geometry the number 1729 is significant enough in that it is the perfect cube of 12 plus 1. However, what is far more arresting is this: in accordance with the numerical values attributed by mystics to individual letters of the Greek alphabet, the number 1729 is the value of the phrase *soma Ieson* which means "body of Jesus".'

As some of the American team of twenty-five were arriving in Turin, the news of Pope John Paul's sudden death was being spread. Ironically one rumour was circulating that the new pope had planned to come quietly to Turin the day he died. He had originally planned to make the visit on 21 September while still Cardinal Archbishop of Venice but the possibility that he was going to go as a pilgrim after being made pope was interpreted by theology professor Alfonso Di Nola of Naples in Italian newspapers as an indication '. . . that nothing has changed, that the church will insist in involving the faithful in these pagan revivals'. It was well known in Turin that Paul VI expected to be at the exposition. The visit was one of two engagements outside Rome to which he had committed himself in the autumn of 1978; the other was to Milan, his former see city.

Visitors coming from the six week exposition were impressed by both the dignity of the showing and the impressive efficiency of the civil and ecclesiastical authorities. Three million visitors were anticipated during the entire period but that figure had been reached by 29 September. The organisers had thought that the greatest numbers would come at the beginning of the event and then this would gradually taper off as the time of the congress neared. The reverse occurred. Over the week-end of 23–24 September more than 200,000 people went to the Cathedral to see the Shroud. Some 150 people fainted or collapsed while queuing. A wait of more than five hours was the norm and visitors were receiving only a brief passing glimpse of the relic.

The situation was quite different when I arrived on 2 September with a group of English visitors, most of whom were Anglican. We had no guarantee of a special viewing and

Father Rinaldi suggested we go to the 7.00 a.m. service of prayers which took place before the queuing crowds were let in. Since a number of our people were elderly I wanted to make certain they knew exactly where to go the next morning and we slowly walked to the cathedral after dinner. To our surprise the evening mass was still in progress and we were allowed to stand at the back of the large congregation. Before us and behind the altar looking like a vast illuminated billboard was the Shroud, looking incredibly white from that distance. This was to be a pleasant prelude for our Sunday morning viewing. The service of matins was tastefully sung. Several nuns helped lead the chanting of psalms and before us the large black framed 'box' containing the centre of everyone's attention. We had been told that this case was filled with inert gas at a pressure slightly higher than normal to keep out harmful bacteria. Constantly circulating piped water monitored by electronic thermocouples and mercury thermometres insured a steady temperature. Close inspection revealed flickering pressure-gauges and hissing pipes. Following the service, we were allowed to pass along the raised walkway which had been built around the Shroud's setting for a closer look. Each successive group of approximately fifteen individuals was permitted to stop before the relic and a member of the group was invited to read in the language of the group a brief explanation of what was before him. There was no prohibition against photography; apparently the container which cost $20,000 was not only bulletproof but also resistant to flash-bulb light.

The lighting from the sides of the container gave the Shroud the appearance of a transparency – it looked as if the light came from the Shroud. One could easily make out the various markings. Creases and patches showed up in a slightly distracting manner in the dramatic lighting scheme. The bloodstains were reddish but the over-all look of the image had that quality of which so many have commented – it blends into the linen deceptively. The cloth looked ancient and fragile, not unlike some of the pharaohs' linens in the neighbouring Turin Egyptian Museum.

Leaving the cathedral the evidence of a well organised crowd control was in progress. Throughout the cathedral our group had noted the large number of volunteer guides and ushers. Many were quite young. More difficult to see were the tough-looking security guards. There was no buying and selling of any mementoes outside. The literature available was handed out free to those entering and leaving the exposition. To one man goes the full credit for the taste with which the event was taking place, the Archbishop. He had ordered a complete ban on all 'profiteering' on the part of the church and the city had followed his example. What literature and photographs pilgrims would desire could be purchased in the shops of the adjacent streets. The money necessary for the essential expenses had come from a special appeal Father Rinaldi and others had launched in America. An anonymous British firm had supplied a loan to pay for the frame.

The Archbishop had taken a special interest in the non-Roman Catholics who were coming to Turin. He had sent our group and the other similar ones which were to follow, his personal greetings and had given permission for holding Anglican masses in the nearby Silesian church of St Maria Ausiliatrice where Don Bosco is buried. The eucharist for our group was to be in the crypt 'chapel of 8,000 relics' (including a portion of the True Cross and a vial of the precious Blood). A most unusual setting for Series II of the Church of England!

The communist mayor of Turin, Diego Novelli, had also taken an interest in the exposition. It was said that over a million pounds had been spent on cleaning Turin's old quarter. Graffiti had been removed, new piping for the Royal Palace gleamed in the sunlight and Guarini's splendid dome to the Royal Chapel was beautifully restored. A series of free concerts and art exhibitions were being presented throughout the six week period. For a city totally unaccustomed to tourism, it was apparent that Turin was learning quickly.

Only one other international congress of sindonology had occurred before the 1978 meeting and that was in Rome twenty-eight years before. The 1939 conference was largely an Italian meeting. The Second International Congress entitled *La Sindone e La Scienza* (the Shroud and Science) opened on Saturday morning at the Istituto Bancario S. Paolo, a banking conference hall, with a chaotic attempt by participants of trying to get through the tight security outside and the lack of organisation inside the doors. There were thirty speakers listed on the programme, two-thirds of whom were Italian. Each of these was allotted fifteen minutes to be followed by a five minute question period. There was no doubt that the congress was to be an Italian affair, and rightly so after all the attention given to the previous Anglo-American gatherings the year before. Most speakers stayed within the given time period and a few absences helped to keep to the time schedule as well as the competent simultaneous translations made into Italian, French and English.

The first speaker, Ian Wilson, presenting his Mandylion theory, was interrupted by the arrival of the Archbishop of Turin who stated that the conference was 'a milestone in understanding the Holy Shroud' and he also pointed to the 'great expectations anticipated by many' as to the discussions which would follow.

Nothing spectacular came from the reports presented. Most of the information was what many had heard and read over the past two years: Dr Bucklin's pathological study, Max Frei's pollen analysis (this time with a complete list of the specimens he had studied), Dr Robinson's previously noted New Testament study and Jackson and Jumper's findings. Several of the Italian speakers had been closely following the studies of the New Mexico conference and added their opinions. Tamburelli presented his computer-enhanced photographs which, he added, suggested that the Shroud face was a 'mass of blood spots'. Professor Claudio Egidi was cautious about the results of his enhancement work but during his question period it was noted that his body image suggested the figure had no navel. The implications of that remark were whispered throughout the hall.

Professor Ettore Morano, electronic microscopic examiner at St Andrew's Hospital at Vercelli, reinforced previously stated remarks that his analyses indicated a great deal of contaminating material on Shroud sample fibres. This information seemed less impressive when much of the same material was seen with the related Egyptian winding sheet fibres which he also investigated. Probably the most eagerly awaited result was that of Dr Alberto Brandone of the ancient University of Pavia. Brandone had been experimenting for some time with a process known as neutron activation. Simply stated the method subjects a sample to neutron bombardment and the atoms it contains, by 'capturing' a neutron and emitting alpha, beta and gamma rays. It is the gamma ray which is then taken into consideration. Each radioactive element emits gamma rays of specific energy, and by identifying and measuring these in the sample, a quantitative analysis of the element can be made. According to Brandone, the detection and measurement of gamma rays was carried out through appropriate crystal detectors of germanium which were connected to a computer-analyser for data processing. With only one single neutron irradiation, more than twenty elements can be found. Brandone's results indicated the high content of gold in his sample (possibly from a previous reliquary) and he more importantly stated that, in his view, 'what is related to blood chemically was not there'.

It would have been difficult not to have noticed the important influence exerted on the congress by Professor Luigi Baima Bollone, Professor of Legal Medicine at the University of Turin. His presentation created one of the strongest debates at the gathering. Bollone claimed that experiments he had made four years ago using aloes and myrrh on the face of a fresh corpse covered with linen, presented an image similar to that of the Turin Shroud. The shading given was that necessary for the later discovered three-dimensionality, as well as the fact that his image did not penetrate the fibres.

Jumper and Jackson and their colleagues kept a noticeable and shrewd low profile at the congress. When listing the 'peculiar' chararacteristics of the Shroud image the fact that 'it fluoresces' was included. No further explanation was given and some of us wondered at the time upon what basis this information had been arrived. The two made a good impression on the participants; it was obvious they were learning some of Father Rinaldi's skilled diplomacy.

A surprising number of speakers and questioners felt the necessity of going on record saying that the Shroud was genuine. By all counts, the 'star speaker' was the leading Spanish Shroud enthusiast, Father Louis Carreño Etxeandia, who exclaimed that the relic 'dripped truth from every fibre' and urged us all to 'just trust in what you see!' Msgr. Ricci, who followed him spoke of the Shroud evidence as 'a gospel written in blood'. Proposals presented by enthusiasts ranged from having a Shroud face placed in all Catholic churches to that of Professor Georges Gharib of the Roman Marianum suggesting the insertion of the Byzantine liturgical texts for the Holy Mandylion be placed in a Roman mass of the Holy Shroud. Interestingly King Umberto was never mentioned at all at the congress – a considerable change from the 1939 and 1950 conferences and the communications from the 1969–73 investigations.

It had been stated in the early stages of the planning for the congress that carbon dating would not be a topic discussed. I had invited Harry Gove to attend the conference with no assurance that he would be able to present his proposal or even discuss it. That was the situation on Sunday morning before John Robinson and I left the Hotel Venezia to walk the three blocks to the congress hall. Robinson had indicated at breakfast that if nothing were said about carbon dating by the time of his talk, he would mention it at the end of his presentation. I had written the 'greetings' from the British Society for the Turin Shroud the night before and had expressed the hope on behalf of the British scientists who had contributed to the analyses of the test proposals their view that carbon dating was the primary test.

Robinson interjected the issue and the door was opened. A prepared statement by Professor Bollone soon followed explaining that the Archbishop had agreed to a series of tests using electromagnetic radiation at various wavelengths but that carbon dating was not 'required or foreseen' (the translator was having difficulty with the exact words used). During the question period which followed Robinson's address, Dr Gove was able to present his views in a deft but necessarily hurried manner. There was no doubt that something important had happened as the television cameras of Canadian Broadcasting and the reporters of *La Stampa* entered the hall.

A further statement was given by Professor Bollone. This time he reiterated the concern over contaminating fungi on cloth samples and repeated what had been said two days previously at a press conference that no 'request' for carbon dating had been received. I was able to face both points during the 'greetings' period which followed: ultrasonic cleaning would remove all contaminants and a proposal had been presented 'not with pride but with love' (as translated by *La Stampa*). I also mentioned the suggestion that, if possible, new samples should be taken during the test period which would shortly occur. This time Don Piero Coero Borga answered. He assured the congress that the 'Raes samples' would not be locked up in the reliquary but would be made available when two laboratories were in agreement in performing the carbon dating by the new method. I was delighted. This was the strongest indication to date of the possibility of carbon dating.

Not many at the congress seemed to be aware of what was to happen that night. As the exposition was coming to a close, the American team, now assisted by some European scientists, were preparing to begin the tests which had been allowed. Many of the Americans had been in Turin for a week planning for what they thought would be a twenty-four hour round of examinations. This had been extended to an additional four days and a reception hall previously used by the Savoyards to greet foreign dignitaries was turned into what Father Rinaldi called 'a control centre for the National Aeronautics and Space Administration'. As the Archbishop celebrated the last mass of the exposition, the final touches were given to the laboratory. Two vital instruments were still held up in Italian customs and Rinaldi was making it clear to the officials in Rome that he would make it public that it was their fault that the Shroud's testing was being delayed.

The Shroud was unceremoniously removed from its complicated frame and taken on a large tray to the laboratory/reception hall. The first examinations were largely photographic, including new pictures taken by Riccardo Bisi and other Italian photographers. Max Frei could be observed quietly entering the side door of the palace prepared to remove more pollen and he was followed by several 'logistics technicians' in blue jeans. The lights stayed on all night in that part of the palace.

Monday morning was Turin's recovery from its greatest influx of tourists to date: 3,330,000. The streets in front of the cathedral were cleaned; the many crowd barriers were removed. The city had an empty look and the cathedral was without its focal point of the past weeks. Absolute security had been dictated by Msgr. Cottino for the test period and those involved were easily identified by the two badges they were required to wear: a blue one with photograph and signature which the Americans had devised themselves and another white one supplied by the custodians of the Royal Chapel.

The first reactions from the examiners were fascinating. Jackson looked as if he had aged ten years having remained in the palace to oversee the first tests for more than twenty-four hours. At the Hotel Sitea, where the American team was staying, Jumper was stating, 'There's no doubt about it – it's a grave cloth!' Vernon Miller who was acting as the head photographer, was remarking about 'all sorts of surprises' they were finding. He also mentioned that it was difficult to focus on the Shroud image at times. As has been previously noted, the closer one gets to an image portion, it seems to disappear and blend into the linen weave. Two other logistics technicians remarked on what many at the exposition had felt, that the blood marks were far more red than the Cordiglia colour photographs seemed to indicate. Thomas D'Muhala, acting as the legal advisor and a logistics manager, quoted John 20.8: '. . . he saw and he believed' as the best description of his initial feelings. It was an irony that the Poor Clares would again be present (as they were after the 1532 fire at Chambery) to unstitch part of the backing cloth for the analysis by a flexible optical instrument. This indicated the first observation the examiners felt free to disclose: the blood images penetrate the cloth and can be observed on the other side.

The Hotel Sitea's lobby reminded one of a doctor's waiting room as exhausted examiners returned for some rest. Kay Jackson was busily 'rounding up' the children of the various participants as Donald Lynn entered the nearby bar. The X-ray fluorescence test had been performed and his reactions were cautious. There had been considerable difficulty in removing some added blue border material (possibly attached in 1973). Lynn expressed a feeling which was to become the rule for what was transpiring – it was going to take a long time to assess the information they were getting.

The bits and pieces of information started to come in fast and furiously:

> You could see the lash marks vividly – like splattered blood! The images – body and blood – do not fluoresce but the background of the Shroud does. The blood marks are definitely different from the body marks – no doubt about it. The blood marks seem to flake. We discovered dirt at one of the footprints! It is quite clear where the Raes' samples were removed and the larger is indeed from the major portion of the cloth. The blood marks clearly go through the other side of the cloth but the body images do not. We want to further explore how linen was made in Jesus' day. The computer broke down but we were able to get all the data gathered, anyway. It's going to take years to assess this material.

Lynn was right and there was no doubt that the next chapters of the Shroud's history would have to be written by scientists.

CHAPTER 8

CAN THIS BE JESUS?

It has been noted frequently that the Turin Shroud is unlike any historical artifact or 'work of art' we know. There is a danger in overstressing this point when we come to analyse the implications of the tests to which it has been subjected. The possibility of its being a forgery of some sort will have to be considered even when all the current scientific analyses are released. Thomas P. F. Hoving, director of New York's Metropolitan Museum of Art,[70] has reminded us that 'the game of duplicity, the fine – or unfine – art of forgery is something that involves everyone in the museum business almost daily'. We are well attuned to the sensational aspects of forgery with the news media revelling in stories of prestigious art galleries being duped by 'master mind' art forgers. There are almost as many varieties of forgery as there are different human personalities – disgruntled painters whose artistic creativity has never been recognised turn on the critics by deceiving them with well executed copies or heretofore unknown 'masterpieces', careful alterations made to 'improve' the quality of an antique for greater sales value and even academic forgery 'jokes' on a grand scale made to impress us with the inventor's creative ability.

Hoving, in a series of talks on 'Art Forgery' at his museum several years ago, stated that there are roughly three major types of forgery:

1. Direct copy as with a neater, smoother, characterless copy of a thirteenth century jewel-encrusted bookcover.

Wealthy tourists know this type well – after a visit to a museum laboratory upon their return home!

2. Pastiche. This is not a new creation but rather a combination of elements from several known and genuine works, not necessarily by the same hand. In 1924 the Burlington Fine Arts Club exhibited a profile portrait of two women which was copied from two existing 'quattrocento' portraits closely related in date. There are many similar examples – some on the walls of important galleries.

3. The last category is the most difficult of all to detect, according to Hoving. 'This is the evocation, when a forger does not go to a single model or several, but tries to pick up the spirit of the time, tries to evoke what an artist would have done.' The works of the talented imitator of Vermeer, Van Meegeren, are in this category.

These are, therefore, the three basic categories of forgery but there can be varied combinations of them. Occasionally there has been an attempt to try a work without any known model or specific historical period such as the 'last words of Moses' written on leather by 'an Egyptian scribe, Unanious', or some relics created for the popular medieval market.

Forging art is far from being a modern phenomenon although our obsession for 'authenticity' and our scientific ability to guarantee it have made it appear so. The sixteenth century art critic and historian, Giorgio Vasari, recorded that while Michelangelo was studying with his teacher, Domenico Ghirlandaio, he was given a head by another artist to copy. Michelangelo performed the task so perfectly that the copy was indistinguishable from the original. '. . . his master took for the original the copy, which Michelangelo returned to him, until he found the boy rejoicing over the success with one of his companions. Afterwards many people compared the two without finding any difference between them.' Forgery is at least five thousand years old. An Egyptian papyrus in the Stockholm museum contains detailed instructions for imitating precious stones in coloured glass. Seneca records that during his lifetime there were several workshops given over to counterfeiting of coloured gems. Vasari also mentions that Michelangelo made a perfect copy of a Greek statue, 'Cupid Asleep', employing what we might think of as a modern technique of 'antiquing' the creation by burying it in the damp earth for a sufficient period of time. The piece was sold as 'classical sculpture' in 1496. Apparently Renaissance man shared a common greed with us for acquiring ancient art! As we saw in Chapter Seven, it has become very difficult for a modern day forger to outwit art dealers and museums now that they employ microchemical and radiation tests in attendant or consulting laboratories. Infrared quickly identifies unique techniques employed by individual artists or earlier sketchings and ultraviolet can detect surface alterations. Microprobes are able to isolate almost every conceivable pigment or chemical which can sometimes show the use of agents not known when the work was supposed to have been executed.

The microanalysis of Dr Walter McCrone on the 'Vinland Map' is a case in point. It was purchased by a New Haven, Connecticut art dealer in 1957 and on the surface looked very impressive: wormholes in the map registered exactly in those of two authentic medieval documents, the Tartar Relation and the Speculum Historiale, indicating to some that it had been at one time bound between these two. Preliminary tests showed that its parchment was genuinely medieval but under ultraviolet light the Vinland Map ink did not react in the same manner as that of the other two documents. It was decided by the new owners of the map, Yale University Library, to have McCrone's laboratory attempt a nondestructive microanalysis. All the ink samples were analysed with the electron microprobe. These were the most minute particles taken from different areas of the parchment. It was evident that the map was a very sophisticated forgery with the only telltale clue being the presence of titanium dioxide pigment which was first synthesised in the 1920's.

Skilled forgers rarely are so foolish as to not employ ancient parchment, linen or old canvas but it is increasingly difficult to stay within the boundaries of pigments used exclusively in certain historical periods. The extensive literature on artists' known preferences for certain pigments as Raphael's characteristic use of walnut oil or Vermeer's favourite blue, costly ultramarine, has made forgery of great masters a considerably complicated and expensive enterprise.

Even with the advanced detection procedures, some decisions on authenticity have never been fully resolved. The celebrated Chalice of Antioch was discovered in 1910 by local Arab labourers digging a well near the traditional site of Antioch's ancient cathedral. Over-zealous estimation of this unusual cup led some to declare that it was the encasement of the Holy Grail. The Antioch Chalice consisted of an inner silver cup set into a beautifully decorated outer cup with two representations of an Apollo-like Christ with his apostles, all encircled by intricate grape vines. The financier, J. P. Morgan, took an interest in it and a long-lasting debate ensued as to its origin and also the questionable circumstances surrounding its discovery. In the chemical analysis executed by Professor Earle R. Caley of Princeton University in 1941 he was not allowed to remove any samples from the chalice and it was impossible to analyse the inner cup which some were suggesting was the cup of the Last Supper. Despite these restrictions, he was able through extensive microscopic examination to conclude: "There is nothing in the general condition of the chalice to indicate that no part of the metal is of modern origin . . . There can be no doubt that this famous chalice is a genuine ancient object.' The Antioch Chalice is catalogued with a *c* AD 400 date by New York's Metropolitan Museum of Art but there is still considerable disagreement for either an earlier or later dating.

Carbon dating has been the most suggested test for the Shroud and has come to be the decisive test for authenticating many historical objects. There was considerable discussion as to the age of the Dead Sea Scrolls after their discovery in the Qumran caves. A violent dispute had broken out in 1949 as to not only the age but also the implications of the writings when they were submitted for examination to the

Oriental Institute in Chicago. Professor Willard Libby was asked to use the carbon dating test on the pieces of linen which had encased the Isaiah scroll. They were burned to ashes and placed into a battery of Geiger-tubes in the manner of the test which Libby had originated and the result was announced that the linen had been made of flax which had been harvested around the time of Jesus. The documents were considered older and after examination by papyrologists a date of *c.* 100 BC was established for the Qumran Isaiah – carbon dating had given the impetus upon which other assessments could be made.

An example where carbon dating results have not been received as settling a question of authenticity is the curious case of 'Noah's Ark'. There is a superficial similarity between the interest in authenticating the Shroud and the fascination held by some for the possibility of Noah's Ark being atop Mt. Ararat in eastern Turkey. Both interests have indomitable enthusiasts, formidable odds with which to contend (the Turin authorities; the reluctance of Turkey to allow full 'foreign' investigation so near the Russian border); the importance for both of radiocarbon-14 dating and the religious implications some see in each pursuit.[71]

It seems to this writer there are some important lessons for future consideration of the Shroud evidence which can be learned from what has happened with the Noah's 'arkeologists' (the nickname given to the enthusiasts by sceptics). Genesis 8.4 states that Noah's great ship rested on the mountains (not mountain) of Ararat. There begins a problem – the possible region includes hundreds of peaks. The Armenians who have lived in the area since the dawn of time, have always felt that the 16,946 foot Mount Ararat is the site. Observations of the 450 ft. long, 45 ft. high, relic are in the writings of the third century BC Babylonian scribe, Berosus. Jacob, Patriarch of Nisbis, tried to reach the spot in AD 330. In 1916 a Russian airman, Captain Roskovitsky, stated that he had sighted a huge ship's hull embedded in a glacier on Mount Ararat. The discovery so impressed the Czar that he sent a team of investigators who were convinced they had located the ark's remains. Photographs and documents attesting to this were supposedly destroyed during the Revolution. Earthquakes in the region in 1883 brought numerous accounts of the ark being seen and in 1974 it was announced that an orbiting American satellite had photographed an 'anomaly' some thought must be the ark.

Almost all of the ark-hunting in recent times has been spear-headed by American fundamentalist groups. There is no mistaking the reason for their exploring: '. . . the very real possibility that in this day when the authority and inspiration of the Bible is being rejected, God may give us proof-positive that one of the greatest historical events in this planet's history is absolutely true.' Not only this but the 'arkeologists' say the discovery of the Ark '. . . would provide conclusive evidence confirming the global nature of the Flood, and thus the mortal blow to any further belief that evolution is a *scientific* theory'.

San Franciscan John Libi says that he has seen the exact site of the ark in a dream and has climbed Ararat seven times, giving up in 1969 when he felt that 73 was too old for such activities. The only tangible evidence to date has been pieces of what has been declared 'hand-hewn' pieces of wood which climbers have found on the mount in areas far above the timber line. The most spectacular piece was discovered by Frenchman Fernard Navarra in 1955. Laboratory tests on the cell structure in Paris and Madrid were said to put the age of this partly fossilised specimen at about 5,000 years (just right by the fundamentalist Biblical account). Radiocarbon dating in Britain and the United States gave a different assessment.

Entry NPL-61 in volume 7 of *Radiocarbon* stated these results for Navarra's wood: 'Oak wood of uncertain species . . . from very large timber structure under ice at 14,000 ft ASL on NW face of Mount Ararat, Turkey. Collected between 1950 and 1955 by Fernand Navarra; submitted by D.H.E. Woodward, Walker and Woodward Ltd. Birmingham . . . *Comment:* evidently not the Ark.' The carbon date given was AD 760; the test had been performed by the

National Physical Laboratory at Teddington. The University of Pennsylvania Radiocarbon Laboratory had arrived at a date of AD 650 with the sample sent to them around the same time as the British test. The results presented a possibility which seemed not to have interested the Noah Ark people. There are Armenian traditions about an ancient shrine high on Ararat – the wood found by Navarra might be from that almost forgotten holy site.

The carbon dating tests have not impaired the enthusiasm of such organisations as 'Search, Inc.' and the Creation Research which have been aided by the publicity of a successful film, 'In Search of Noah's Ark'. Reaction on their part to the C-14 tests was not surprising: 'The ages of the samples of wood returned by several experts reveal only the unreliability of the dating methods . . . its results are no longer taken seriously by objective scientists.'

Considering the foregoing objects, the Shroud's study has involved an unparalleled number of disciplines in judging its claims: pathology, anatomy, New Testament scholarship, historical criticism and the most modern scientific scrutiny and investigating techniques. No historical artifact or art object has been subjected to such a barrage of examination. There is no artifact quite comparable to it, but there are other important relics enshrined by the Roman Catholic church.

The realm of 'other relics' is one which most persons interested in the Shroud would prefer to avoid and so, as an Anglican, perhaps I can interject it with no one feeling I have a 'vested interest' in the matter. The understandable desire of many has been to divorce the Turin Shroud from the tainted history and practice of relics but the fact remains that it is a relic and in some sense must be considered and judged as such.

At the Benedictine Abbey of Argenteuil near Versailles there is a 'holy cloak' thought to be the seamless garment woven for Jesus by his mother. It is first mentioned in a twelfth century document of uncertain value and was apparently brought to Argenteuil by Charlemagne. Dr Barbet referred to the garment in his book and gave the information that infrared photographs of it made by a friend in 1934 had revealed bloodstains in the same anatomical areas as the Shroud. Attempts made to find out more about this 'testing' have proven fruitless. The authorities at Argenteuil have kept an even greater silence about their relic than Turin with the 1969 investigations.

Another 'holy garment' found at Trier, Germany claiming to be Christ's seamless robe (as described in John 19.23), supposedly discovered by the great relic-collector, St Helena, has been favoured over other claims through the centuries because of the city's Roman and early Christian origins. This garment was first exhibited publicly in 1512 and almost two million pilgrims saw it in 1959. Recent excavations at Trier have indicated the knowledge of the relic's existence from early times of this important ancient city's records. Johann Ronge, the subsequent founder of a German Catholic sect strongly attacked the Bishop of Trier in 1844 for his exposition of the garment. There was an investigation of the condition of the cloth in 1974. It was not possible to ascertain how much of the felt-like coat might be considered the original relic. It might prove to be useful to have these two relics studied in relationship to the Shroud as with the already mentioned Oviedo linen. The difficulty with these relics is that the authorities in charge of them seem overly reluctant to make public any of the investigations which have occurred. It has been a quiet policy of ecclesiastics in charge of such treasures to have them secretly (and frequently inadequately) tested and then, if the results turn out to be rather negative, they slowly but surely 'phase-out' the objects from active devotional practice. The Vatican was much more public about the results of its 'Chair of St Peter' which was carbon dated to be of a much later date than the first pope. The 'Shroud-related' articles might present some valuable information if they could be studied in a scientific atmosphere.

The Turin Shroud has been singled out as being unlike any artifact, work of art or relic that we know. We have seen a wealth of information which presents it as a formidable document:

1. In relationship to the Gospel accounts of the death and burial of Jesus, it demonstrates that Jesus was scourged in the Roman manner; he wore a unique caplike 'crown' of thorns; he was nailed through the wrists (not unlike the archaeological evidence of the only crucified remains ever found); his bones were not broken, his side was pierced by a lance and he was buried in a sepulchre, not burnt to ashes. In other words, all these points of the Shroud correspond to the Biblical account in a reasonable manner.

2. The linen of the Shroud could date from the time of Christ, according to expert analysis.

3. No pigments have been traced on the image and it appears as totally superficial corresponding to what seems to be the action of a short-blast, high intensity radiation, or some sort of photographic process.

4. The imprints of the Shroud body are anatomically correct.

5. The body is naked and bruised, which was not the manner of depicting Christ in early Christian art (even replicas of the Shroud until fairly recently placed a loin cloth over the buttocks and genital area).

6. The image is best seen when photographed on a negative plate. This positive-negative principle of photography was unknown until fairly recent times.

7. The image has three-dimensionality 'programmed' into it, and it is fairly well agreed that whatever created the image worked at a distance instead of by direct contact.

8. Pollen analysis has indicated that there is the possibility of pollen on the Shroud from the time of Jesus.

When faced with those points, some have suggested that it wasn't necessary to go any further in testing the Shroud. When compared with archaeological and art objects such as those we have noted in this chapter, the Shroud has already 'passed' as thorough an examination as given to others. Joseph Hanlon writing for the *New Scientist* pointed out that the biggest arguments against fraud is that the Shroud is simply too good'. Then he went on to ask, 'But could there have been a double fake, one in the fourteenth century and another in the last century?[72] Professor of German at the University of London, G. A. Wells, has reminded that '. . . it is very difficult to write a technical history of forgery in the way one can write a history of the techniques of shipbuilding. Forgers and magicians are not given to publishing the secrets of their craft, and a modern scientist is not in a good position to say what knowledge and technical resources were available to a forger in the Dark and Middle Ages. One thing, however, can be taken for granted – that men were then as inventive, ingenious, dishonest and acquisitive as they are now.'[73] There will always be this type of conjecture but carbon dating should be able to at least 'de-fuse' some of the suggestions.

The tests which were performed 8–13 October 1978, once the results are fully assessed – should further eliminate certain options as to the image creation process. But Ray Rogers has wisely urged caution on this point, 'If we eliminate all the natural ways that an image can be produced, then it will make a pretty strong case for something that could not be done by human agency. I wouldn't want to go any further than that.'

Science is not a process of proving things but building probabilities and some of us at the October Congress were not pleased by views expressed which seemed to be saying that science could prove the Shroud to be genuine. As Ian Wilson and I waited for Donald Lynn to return to the Hotel Sitea between working shifts, a member of the Christ Brotherhood who was travelling with the American team asked us our views on what was happening in Turin. This 'Jesus cult' group, which was until recently stationed at Santa Fe, New Mexico (they have moved to Colorado) has had a considerable interest in the Shroud. As far back as 1976 Lynn and Jean Lorre of the Jet Propulsion Laboratory had been approached by one of their members, Tom Dolle, to see whether it was possible to use some of the techniques they had employed in enhancing images of Earth, Mars, Venus and Mercury to images of the Shroud. The Christ Brotherhood was present at the New Mexico conference. The member who talked with Wilson and me was quite surprised to discover that a clergyman like myself was not in favour of using the Shroud evidence for evangelistic purposes. This same desire was repeated by other representatives at the congress. One Armenian even suggested that the carbon dating be delayed for a few years so that the 'Shroud's story' could be used to convert the unchurched.

An attempt to use what science has said about the Shroud to date to confirm the existence, death and resurrection of Jesus is not only questionable but goes directly against a faith which does not ask for or need signs – indeed disdains them in the gospels. I heartily agree with fellow American Episcopal priest and Los Alamos physical chemist, Robert Dinegar, when he remarks, 'I can see no way how a one-to-one correspondence between the Shroud image and Jesus can be certified. This particular identification can come only through the eyes of faith, not from the witness of impartial data.'[74]

There will always be the *possibility* that the image on the Shroud is that of an early Christian martyr – *perhaps* it represents a mock crucifixion as has been suggested by Professor Pier Angelo Gramaglia of the Turin Seminary. The Turin Shroud should never be used as a kind of 'Exhibit A' for the faith. No Christian's faith should ever rest upon the evidence of a piece of linen any more than it was necessary, according to Jesus, for Thomas to see the marks in his hands or the wound in his side.

What many suspected a long time ago when the Shroud was first seriously considered remains the case – the more the Shroud was studied, the more questions it would raise. I suspect that there are some big surprises and mysteries yet to come.

CHAPTER NOTES AND REFERENCES

Chapter 1

1. Pierre Barbet in *A Doctor at Calvary* (Doubleday & Co., New York, 1963) pointed out that there are a number of exceptions to the rule in art of having the nails piercing the palms. There is a Rubens painting in Rijk Museum and three Van Dycks (at Antwerp, Brussels and Bruges) all showing a piercing through the wrist area as with the Shroud. Barbet also refers to a large ivory crucifix given by the Knights of St John of Jerusalem to Pope Pius XI which indicates the same.

   Professor Umberto Fasola of the Pontifical Commission of Archaeology mentioned a crucifixion graffito at the October Congress which he stated was found in 1959 in Roman ruins by Professor Maiuri Amedeo which showed nailing through the wrists.

2. Some writers have questioned this generally accepted estimate of height (Msgr. Giulio Ricci in particular). The difficulty in measurement comes with how much should be allowed for the bend of the knees and high up the top of the head are calculated.

   According to the research of Professor Luigi Baimar Bollano, of the University of Turin, 180cm. is not an unusual height in the Jewish world of that time. In fact, he writes, in those areas where the Semitic ethnic group maintained its characteristics, for example, in the valleys of Yemen, it is not uncommon to meet persons that size. In addition, in the Jewish necropolis of Giv'at ha-Mivtar in Jerusalem, skeletons from the first century after Christ have been found, among them three skeletons of tall men.

Chapter 2

'Concise Helps to the Study of the Bible', *The Oxford Self-Pronouncing Bible* (Oxford University Press, 1960).

The Greek word used for hand, *cheir*, in the gospels can indicate any area from the forearm down.

Cf. *Tos. San.* 9. 8 ed. Zuckermandel, p. 429. The Jewish custom of burying all human beings – slaves, pagans and criminals differs noticeably from the Roman practice of depriving executed criminals of burial. In *Semahot* 2.13, it is related that those who were martyred on the cross by the Romans were exposed till their flesh wasted away.

In some artistic representations of the crucifixion, the lance thrust is depicted as occurring on the left side because of the heart's position. Rembrandt who is known for documenting details in many of his paintings, shows the piercing on the right side as is the case with the Shroud.

H. Daniel-Rops, the French Biblical scholar, offers an interesting explanation for the position on the right: 'The right hand thrust was the classic manoeuvre of Roman sword drill since the left side would, in combat, be covered by the shield.' (*Jesus and His Times* (New York, 1954)).

Some writers, including Ian Wilson, have made a point that the shape of the wound ($1\frac{3}{4}$ by $\frac{7}{16}$ in. wide) would indicate the use of the Roman *lancea*. Wilson states, 'From excavated examples, the shape of the lancea's blade corresponds exactly to the shape of the elliptical wound visible on the Shroud. It is another strikingly authentic, and

Roman, detail.' *(The Turin Shroud*, Gollancz, London, 1978).
7. Anthony Sava, 'The Wound in the Side of Christ', *Catholic Biblical Quarterly*, XIX, No. 3 (July 1957).
8. Geza Vermes, *Jesus The Jew* (Collins, London, 1973).
9. Henry Latham has given in *The Risen Master* (Cambridge 1905) this description of what Jesus' tomb possibly looked like:

'Just beyond the walls of Jerusalem there is a mass of limestone rock rising somewhat abruptly from the surface. Out of this a cave has been hollowed to serve as a tomb; at the entrance to which the rock has been cut away, leaving the face comparatively smooth, and perpendicular to the ground. The doorway of the tomb is an aperture about two feet broad and something under four feet high. Past the base of this, on the ground, there runs a furrow grooved out of the rocky soil. This is an inch or two deep and ten or twelve inches broad. Along this furrow, backwards and forwards past the door of the tomb, rolls a massive disc of stone, much like a grindstone of four feet diameter, which serves as a door; it stands on its edge close against the rock, so that, when it is opposite to the doorway, it closes the aperture, and when it is rolled to the end of the furrow it leaves it free. The cave penetrates seven or eight feet into the rock; on one side of the doorway, as you enter, there is a low recess, nearly as long as the cave and two and a half feet broad. The base of this recess is a ledge of the native rock, upon which the body was to be laid. This ledge has a low step in it, at about a foot and a half from the far end of the recess: the raised slab so formed is meant to serve as a pillow for the head of the corpse.'

10. It is not clear whether the full ceremonial washing was allowed on the Sabbath.
11. A. P. Bender, *Jewish Quarterly Review*, 1894–95.
12. Excavations of Christians buried in Egypt between AD 130 and 500 showed internment in a variety of clothes; several shrouds, ordinary clothing, shrouds with or without face veils, ribbons binding ankles and wrists and single

shroud burials like those of the Jewish poor in Israel before and after Jesus' time. (Maurus Green, OSB, 'Enshrouded in Silence', *Ampleforth Journal* (Autumn 1969)).
13. From a presentation by Dr Robinson at the Symposium on the Turin Shroud, London, 17 September 1977.
14. The Reverend Bernard Orchard, OSB, of Ealing Abbey, London interprets the identity of the sudarion in a different manner: 'In my view, the sindon of the Synoptics is the Shroud itself. I also accept the genuineness of Luke 24.12, and this means that Luke distinguished the *sindon* and the *othonia*, just as John does.

Hence I think the balance of probability is that the Synoptic sindon is John's *sudarion*. It is a perfect description of the Shroud to say that it was a "sweat sheet" and that it "was over his head" (John 20.7). True it is impossible to prove absolutely but I think it is the natural interpretation. The "jaw-band" which Robinson speaks of could be, and in my view more likely to be, one of the othonia; and it does look as if there was such a jaw-band. But I do not think that the "jaw-band" was the *sudarion*. I think that Robinson's imagination is here running away with itself!'
15. Henry Latham alludes to an interpretation of the covering of the linen cloths which creates a problem of identifying them with the Turin Shroud: He refers to Eldersham (Life And Times Of Jesus The Messiah) who 'is a good authority', but as others tell us 'we have but scanty information about the funeral usages of the Jews in our Lord's time'. According to Edersheim (Vol. I p. 556): 'The face of the dead body was uncovered. The body lay with its face turned upwards, and its hands folded on the breast.' Latham after observing 'existing usage' in the Middle East, felt that 'the neck and the upper surface of the shoulders were commonly left bare as well as the face'.

Dr Eric M. Meyers, Professor of New Testament at Duke University, North Carolina, USA, who has written definitive analyses of Jewish ossuaries for the Biblical

Institute of Rome, has expressed a similar note: 'There is one interesting point to be explored further, that is the nature of the purported shroud and its terminology. The *sindon/othonia* juxtaposition has a parallel in Hebrew sources, *tachrichin/kliva*. What these things actually looked like is difficult, but I can't infer from any source that the face was covered by a cloth of any kind. I understand the wrapping of the face *(periededeto)* with a napkin *(sudarion)* to be around the neck with the face exposed. This is still the custom in traditional Jewish circles.'

16. Henry Latham's account of what the apostles saw as recorded in St John is an interesting interpretation of the evidence:

'In this recess, on the lower part of the ledge, lay the grave-clothes. They were in no disorder, they were just as they were when Joseph and others had wrapped them round the body of the Lord, only they were lying flat, fold over fold, for the body was gone. On the raised part of the ledge at the far end, all by itself, was the napkin that had gone round the head: this was not lying flat, but was standing up a little, retaining the twirled form which had been given it when it had been twined round the head of the Lord. Nothing in the place gave any sign of the touch of human hands: the body had been embedded in the powdered aloes and myrrh, but of this there was not a trace; the spice remained enclosed by the "cloths" between which it had been placed when the body was laid on the slab. Something which the scene conveyed may have gone to the hearts of Peter and John; at any rate we can see that when they went out, they were not in the frame of mind that they had been in when they reached the tomb. I think that the impression stole over them, as they scrutinised what they saw, that "God was in that place". This is not too dissimilar to the accounts of the Buddhist holy men.

17. The Reverend Jasper White, WF, has presented an arousing theory about what happened to the Shroud after Jesus' resurrection (*The Tablet* 30 Sept. 1978). '. . . what

sort of clothes did Jesus wear on Easter Day? Were they ethereal or of earthly texture? If the latter, where did Jesus get them? Remember: all four evangelists insist that on Calvary his clothes were taken from him. The two images on the shroud confirm this fact. Well, here is one guess. When Jesus rose (de-died, as we say in Swahili) and left the closed tomb he took the *sindon* (shroud) with him, throwing it round him like a toga (cf. Peter leaving prison. Acts 1.2,8). The photo prints inside the shroud were set and dry.

No evangelist mentions the shroud in the tomb on Easter morn, because *it was no longer there* – as simple as that! The *othonia* (bandages) were there and so was the *sudarion* (the jaw-band), but not the *sindon*. Jesus was wearing it!'

18. Col P. W. O'Gorman, CMD, MD, 'The Holy Shroud of Jesus Christ: New Discovery of the Cause of the Impression', *Ecclesiastical Review* (Philadelphia, 1940).

19. Chogyam Trungpa, *Born In Tibet* (Allen and Unwin, London, 1966).

20. The stigmatic and mystic, Anne Catherine Emmerick (born 1774), wrote down her experience in 1820 with the help of a poet, Clemens Brentaro in *The Dolorous Passion of Our Lord Jesus Christ*. Her description of the entombment and subsequent miracle which followed is remarkable in relationship to the Shroud, 'the sacred body of Jesus, with all its wounds, appeared imprinted upon the cloth which covered it, as though he had been pleased to reward their care and their love, and leave them a portrait of himself through all the veils with which he was enwrapped. With tears they embraced the adorable body, and then reverently kissed the wonderful impression which it had left. Their astonishment increased when, on lifting up the sheet, they saw that all the bands which surrounded the body had remained white as before, and the upper cloth alone had been marked in this wonderful manner. It was not a mark made by the bleeding wounds, since the whole body was wrapped up and covered with sweet spices, but it was a supernatural portrait, bearing testimony to the divine creative power ever abiding in the body of Jesus.'

Chapter 3

21. In correspondence, Avery said, 'I wonder if you think this dedication was in mind when the sculptor or patron was designing the scene of the entombment of Christ? I would say that the cloth in which Christ is being laid to rest does receive unusual prominence.'
22. M. Andre Perret, *Histoire de Saint Suiare du XIV au XVI Siècle* (Turin, 1960).

    There are some accounts (Hubert Cole *The Black Prince* (1976) and Lingard/Belloc *History of England*) which indicate that Geoffrey was not the 'knightly ideal' in his involvement with the bribery of the governor of Calais, Amerigo, and the latter's subsequent execution.
23. The Shroud remained at Roche St Hippolyte for thirty-four years and was shown to the faithful annually in a large field called the *pratum domini* (meadow of the Lord). This is usually the name for a field given to the church for the express purpose of growing wheat and grapes for the mass.
24. Their report can be read in R. P. Eschbach *La Saint Suare De Nostre Seigneur* (Turin, 1915).

    The Poor Clares kept the Shroud for seventeen days and it was stretched in a frame during the repairing with four guards holding lighted candles before the relic. People were allowed to see the nuns at work from time to time and it is known that they backed the linen with holland cloth before the patching began. Princess Clotilde of Savoy provided a crimson lining in 1868.

    Almost as great a danger to the Shroud came in the 1500s from the continuous warfaring that covered the area. On one occasion the relic was taken from Chambery through the Ala valley and Turin to Milan and Nizza. It travelled back to Vercelli and then was restored to Chambery when peace was finally restored. After such wanderings in the middle of open warfare, it is amazing that the relic escaped damage and theft.

5. In early September 1939 the Shroud secretly left Turin and was taken to safety in the isolated monastery of Montevergine in southern Italy. It was feared that the bombings around and in Turin might damage it or that the Nazis might steal it.

On 7 September the Shroud was placed in an ordinary box and taken to Rome by train and then by car to Montevergine where only two superiors of the Benedictine order were told what the box contained. It was hidden under a side altar in the chapel of the monastery. The Shroud remained there for seven years. When the Germans arrived in Turin, Cardinal Fossati informed them that the cloth belonged to the Savoy family and that they had removed it from its usual place of keeping. The Shroud returned to Turin in October 1946 after being shown to the unsuspecting monks of Montevergine. Turin felt that the war was really over when it was brought back.

6. Zazimir de Proszynski, *The Authentic Photograph of Christ* (London, 1932) (source: *De Vir. Illust.* Chapter ii.) Not many commentators have taken this account seriously. The latest edition of Hennecke's *New Testament Apocrypha* sees the linen cloth mentioned as a 'legendary working up of the resurrection story'. One cannot help but admire Hugh Schonfield's life-long attempt to have this gospel, among other apocryphal literature, taken more seriously by New Testament scholars who, in the main, seem ready to simply reiterate former German judgments as having settled the matter once and for all time. We do not have to accept Schonfield's conclusions in his rather sensational works like *The Passover Plot* to share his conviction that many scholars seem 'fearful of what truths might reside in such works'. When I visited him in London, he stood by his 1932 writing and gave the impression of an undaunted explorer despite his age and the heavy criticism hurled upon his writings.

27. *La Conquete De Constantinople*, ed. Lauer (Paris, 1924).

Another edition is from *Historiens Et Chroniquers Du Moyen Age*, ed. Pauphilet (Paris, 1952).

The text in the latter reads: 'Et entre ces autres en eut un autre des monstiers, que on apeloit madame Sainte Marie de Blakerne, où li sydoines là où Notre Sire fu envelopoés, y estoit, qui chascun vendredi se dressoit tous drois, si que on y povoit bien voir la figure Nostre Seigneur; ne ne seut on onques, ne Grien ne François, que cist sydoines devint quant la ville fu prise.'

28. Dom Sylvester Houédard, OSB, has pointed out that as Robert de Clari 'brought back (if not the *whole* great chest of relics at Corbie as stated in the inventory – post-1285) at least the crystal crucifix with a fragment of the Shroud. I still wonder if perhaps he knew more than he said and maybe he helped to get the Shroud out of Constantinople.'

29. Besides the Besançon Shroud there have been a number of others which have been revered as Jesus' burial garment. The Cadouin Winding Sheet was supposedly sent by a Caliph to Charlemagne and was venerated for many years but it was discovered that it was decorated with phrases from the Koran in 1945!

The even more ancient shroud of Compiègne was also reputed to be a gift to Charlemagne and his grandson presented it to the monks of Compiègne in 877. This relic was the object of large pilgrimages and much Papal and episcopal patronage until its destruction in the French Revolution.

30. Paul de Gail, *S. J. Histoire Religieuse Du Linceul Du Christ* (Editions France-Empire, Paris, 1973).

The Edessa Image is identified as the 'sanctam toellam tabulae infertam' in Baldwin's Golden Bull according to Runciman and De Riant. The end for the image came in 1792 with the sacking of the Saint Chapelle by revolutionaries, in their estimation.

31. A link with Cyprus has been put forward by many

writers of the Shroud's possible early history. One tradition mentioned by seventeenth century Italian writers maintained that the Shroud was kept in Jerusalem and Syria until 1087, when Patriarch Heraclius gave it to the Kings of Cyprus. The evidence that Geoffrey I de Charny visited Cyprus with Philip of Mezieres during the campaign of 1343-1346 has led to the conjecture that the king of Cyprus gave it to them for the king of France on that occasion. Maurus Green, OSB, has referred to 'an assumption, taken for granted by both defenders and opponents of the Turin Shroud, that the shroud of Lirey, condemned by Bishop d'Arcis in 1389 as a forgery, was identical with the cloth of Turin'. When I pressed him why he had made such a remark, he responded by saying, 'What started me doubting was the Cyprus tradition'. Duke Louis (to whom Margaret de Charny had presented the Lirey shroud) was married to the Cypriot princess, Anne. The sixteenth century historians, Adomo and Pingone, recorded the idea that the Duke had obtained the Shroud through his wife. This has led to the idea that perhaps Pierre d'Arcis was right in describing the Lirey shroud as a representation in that Duke Louis had the true shroud from Cyprus and had obtained its copy from Margaret in order to expose the original without a rival.

32. One intriguing possibility of an early representation of the Shroud was brought to my attention by John McInally of Worcester Park, Surrey who noted a carved gem in the September 1902 issue of *Harper's Monthly Magazine*. The gem is listed as 'A True Portrait of the Holy Sudarium' and is dated second century AD. It shows a group of clergy and soldiers holding what looks like a seventeenth or eighteenth century representation of the Turin Shroud – the loins are covered. The gem was portrayed in a collection and study by Maxwell Sommerville, Professor of Glyptology at the University of Pennsylvania.

33. That lovely old volume, Frederic W. Farrar's *The Life of Christ As Represented In Art* (London, 1894) points out this relationship: 'To the eyes of a Greek or Roman the

figure of the Good Shepherd differed but little from that of Apollo Nomios or Aristeus, Apollo feeding the flocks of Admetus; or from the celebrated statue of Hermes Kriophoros (the ram-bearer) at Tanagra. It also recalled in some instances the figure of Orpheus.'

34. Sir Steven Runciman, 'Some Remarks on the Image of Edessa', *Cambridge Historical Journal,* iii (1931).

35. According to Runciman (op. cit.), there was a curious change in nomenclature for the Edessa Image. 'During the iconoclastic controversy the Greek authors, though they knew that the image was a piece of our Lord's cloth, called it simply an icon. Now they all mentioned it as the "Mandylion", while the contemporary Arabi writers called it the *mandil. Mandil* was a word long engrained in the Arabic language, though probably it was originally derived from the Latin *Mantile* or *Mantilium,* our "mantle".'

36. H. C. Bowen, *Ali Ibn-Isa* (Cambridge, 1928).

37. In another account in *The Teaching of Addai* ed. G. Phillips (London, 1876) it is stated that King Abgar's emissary, Hannan, 'painted the portrait with choice colours', as we have previously noted.

38. Jacques de Molay brought a vast hoard of treasures from Cyprus to Paris (including twelve horseloads of gold and silver) when he was called to answer charges against the order at the bidding of the French king in 1307.

39. The slight difference in spelling seems unimportant to Wilson. There were many such variances, but no genealogical link has been established despite numerous enquiries.

40. The Edessa Image was mentioned by several sources as being in the great collections of the Byzantines: William of Malmesbury, William of Tyre, Anthony of Novgorod and others. Their lists are given in De Riant, *Exuviae Sacrae Constantinopolitanae,* ii, 211 ff. Robert de Clari calls it a *touaile* in his inventory of relics.

41. In his *Icons* (Faber and Faber, London, 1963), Konrad Onasch relates how the icon artist 'had to master the allegorical measurements of figures, as for example of the circle, and to represent the *homo allegoricus,* the allegor-

ical man, in relation to eternity . . . The circle, for instance, as the allegorical figure-measure of the infinite is used for the proportions of the head . . . We take as an example the icon of the 'Saviour painted without hands . . .' The details of the measurements of the head and its outlines are fixed by three circles, which have a common centre right at the bridge of the nose. The radius of the first circle is equal to it; this circle determines the height and width of the front as well as the starting line of the hair. The second circle, the radius of which measures two nose-lengths, determines the height of the head and the point of the chin, and outlines the head. The third circle, with a radius of three nose-lengths, leads through the pit of the throat and outlines the halo. Almost all heads and faces of saints in icons are proportioned according to this picture of Christ; according to the allegorical conception of the world of Pseudo Dionysius . . .'

42. A. N. Grabar, *History Of The Ikon Of The Saviour Not-Made-By-Hands Of The Cathedral In Laon* (Prague, 1930).

43. During the last phase of the Byzantine Empire, the *epitaphioi* appear. In the words of John Beckwith, '. . . in view of the imminent demise of the Empire it is meet and just that those equivalents to a pall or shroud should still exist.' These embroidered linens had depictions of the dead Christ, either on the shroud or the stone of anointing. The body was usually nimbed with a cross halo and wrapped in a loin cloth. The wounds on the hands and feet and in the side were displayed clearly. Despite the subject matter, as was usual with the Eastern depiction of Christ's passion and death and burial, the tone admitted no emotion (*Early Christian and Byzantine Art* (Penguin books, 1970)).

According to Pauline Johnstone of the Victoria and Albert Museum, her reading of the complicated history of the *epitaphios* does not suggest that this particular veil was ever connected with the actual shroud of Christ. 'On the contrary it seems to have been strictly related to the elements of the Eucharist and only in the fourteenth century thought of as representing the earthly body of Christ. On the other hand, the Early Fathers did apparently make a symbolic comparison between the altar cloth called the *eiliton* and the fair linen of Joseph of Arimathea but I have not seen it suggested that the connection was regarded as anything more concrete than a starting point for mystical thought' (private correspondence). Mrs Johnstone's *The Byzantine Tradition in Church Embroidery* (Tiranti, London, 1967) is a valuable source of information.

In the Eastern Orthodox liturgy for Holy Week the *epitaphios* was used on Good Friday and Easter Eve to cover the ceremonial bier of Christ. The faithful venerated the embroidered figure of the dead Christ on the cloth and the mood was definitely one of mourning as can be vividly seen with the later additional figures added to the cloth of the Virgin and St John and attendant angels. This element of mourning was clearly connected with the sacrament of the Eucharist, according to John Beckwith.

44. Ernle Bradford, *The Great Betrayal* (Hodder & Stoughton, London, 1967).

Chapter 4

45. John Walsh's *The Shroud* (W. H. Allen, London, 1964) remains the most informative book in English on this period of the Shroud's history.
46. Luigi Fossati, 'On an Alleged Reply . . .' *Sindon* (March 1960).
47. This exposition was to commemorate what was thought to be the 1900th anniversary of Jesus' death.
48. Robert Bucklin, MD, FACP, The Legal And Medical Aspects Of The Trial And Death Of Christ, *Medicine, Science And The Law* (London, January 1970).
49. Geoffrey Ashe, 'What Sort of Picture?' *Sindon*, (1966).

50. John Hersey, *Here To Stay* (Bantam Books, New York 1963).
51. *The British Journal Of Photography*, 30 June 1967.
52. *Israel Exploration Journal* (20), 1970.
53. *The Catholic Herald*, 18 March 1960.

Chapter 5

54. David Friedrich Strauss, *New Life Of Jesus*, i. 412 (London, 1879).
55. All quoted material is from literature supplied to the author by the Ahmadiyya group: *Jesus In India* by Hazrat Mirza Ghulam Ahmad, Ahmadiyya Muslim Foreign Missions Dept, Rabwah, Pakistan and *Death On The Cross?* by Abul Atta Jalandhri, The London Mosque.
56. Rodney Hoare, *The Testimony Of The Shroud* (Quartet Books, London, 1978) and an earlier prospectus, *Proof Positive*.
57. Bucklin's views were given in private correspondence.

Chapter 6

58. A useful book on the last days of the reigns of Victor Emmanuel III and his son, Umberto II, is Robert Katz's *The Fall Of The House Of Savoy* (George Allen and Unwin Ltd., London, 1972). Denis Judd's *Eclipse Of Kings* (Macdonald and Jane's, London, 1976) has some rather 'spicy' material on Umberto's private life and that of his children. According to The *Sunday Times* (20 August 1978) Umberto's son '. . . was charged yesterday (19

August) by a Corsican magistrate with deliberate wounding and carrying a loaded firearm. He has now been placed in custody on the Mediterranean island. The charges follow an incident last week in which Dirk Hamer, a 19-year-old German student, was seriously wounded in the groin when shot with a rifle at Cavallo Island.'

59. David Willis, 'False Prophet and Holy Shroud', *The Tablet* 13 June 1970.
60. Peter Rinaldi, 'Turin and the Holy Shroud' in *Proceedings Of The 1977 U.S. Conference Of Research On The Shroud Of Turin*, Holy Shroud Guild, New York, 1977. 294 East 150, N.Y., N.Y. 10451.

The results of the 1969 and 1973 investigations are to be found in a supplement of the *Rivista Diocesan Torinese* published in January, 1976 under the title, *La S. Sindone*. A highly critical study of these results was made by the International Centre of Sindonology in 1977, *Osservazioni Alle Perizie Ufficiali Sulla Santa Sindone*, 1969–1976.

61. According to Ian Wilson (op. cit.), examples of the more complex three-to-one twill are known from the time of Christ but in silks rather than linen. 'Silk examples, thought to be of Syrian manufacture, have been found at Palmyra (dated before AD 276), and in a child's coffin (c. AD 250) excavated at Holborough, Kent, England.'
62. There is considerable disagreement as to whether the side strip which runs the entire length of the Shroud was an original part of the relic. Prof. Raes stated that there was little difference between the two samples, except for the absence of cotton in the one from the side strip. Some writers in the past entertained the notion that this strip replaced the portion of the relic given to St Louis in 1247. Paul de Gail fully investigates this in his previously noted volume, but he arrives at no firm conclusion as to when the strip was added.
63. Yigael Yadin, *Bar-Kokhba* (Random House, New York, 1971).
64. Dr Frei has supplied me with this information. Some of the material was reported at the London Symposium on

the Shroud, 16–17 Sept. 1977. Dr Stuart Fleming, formerly at the Research Laboratory for Archaeology, Oxford, has stated that he and his colleagues do not see how Frei can substantiate his claims beyond indicating that the pollen spectrum matches perhaps a half millennium in antiquity.

There is another difficulty in Frei's assertions. Analysing the ancient and modern plant life of Israel is complicated by its extraordinary variety. The countryside between Jerusalem and the Dead Sea is linked with four distinct areas of the earth's surface. Where there is the most rainfall around Jerusalem the plants belong to the flora of the Mediterranean. As any tourist knows, much of this landscape is like Italy. Go four kilometres from Jerusalem and one is in a treeless steppe which is similar to the vast Anatolian steppe from which Frei also found specimens. How different the flora of Edessa, the known home of the Mandylion, was from this area is a question. Many botanists I have talked with think Frei can not be so definite as even to suggest that his Anatolian specimens can give Wilson the right to say, 'Frei's evidence also corroborates the author's theory that the Shroud and the Mandylion are the same' (op. cit. p. 206).

The Dead Sea desert region is linked with the flora and fauna of the Sahara and Arabia; the Rift Valley and the area around Jericho has many elements also to be found in the eastern Sudan. As John Wilkinson has written in a volume I found extremely interesting for this discussion, *Jerusalem As Jesus Knew It* (Thames and Hudson, London, 1978): 'No region . . . in the Middle East boasts so wide a variety of climate and environment.'

At his presentation to the Congress on 7 October, Prof. Frei stated he was able to identify 48 plants, 16 of which grew in France and Italy, but 21 were identified as desert plants growing in saline areas like those near the Dead Sea. Of the list he presented at the Congress, 13 were listed as coming specifically from the Jerusalem area and nowhere else and 14 were possibly from the area of Jerusalem and the area around northern Syria. Only one was specifically designated as from the Urfa (Edessa) area alone. Frei could also state at this time that he found no other elements from his tests on the samples giving any idea as to possible age.

65. The *Sunday Times*, 10 and 17 April 1977.

66. Readers interested in fuller discussion of Jumper and Jackson's findings as well as those of their colleagues should read the Conference *Proceedings* available from the Holy Shroud Guild of New York. Material quoted from these proceedings is from this document.

67. Searching through the British Museum's vast numismatic collection for possible 'candidates' of the indicated size, it was apparent that the most likely types would be leptons – the so-called 'widow's mite'. In particular, a lepton of Pontius Pilate coined in AD 30–31 seems to be of almost exact proportions. Leptons of this period did not carry peculiarly Roman insignia. In fact, most of them were imprinted with palm fronds and would have been acceptable to an orthodox Jew.

68. Much of my material concerned with Dr McCrone's laboratory and methods as well as the discussion on carbon dating comes from material he has supplied me in my involvement with the test possibilities over the past few years. Helpful articles on radiocarbon testing by newer methods can be found in: *New Scientist*, 13 Oct, 1977; *Revue De Physique Appliquee* (Tome 12), 12 Oct, 1977; *Physics Today*, Dec, 1977. An article by Walter McCrone on small particle analysis appeared in the July 1976 issue of *Analytical Chemistry*.

Chapter 7

I am indebted to Father Rinaldi, Walter McCrone, John Jackson, and Harry Gove for much of the information of this chapter. Two invaluable papers were: 'Proposal For Investigating The Shroud Of Turin By Electromagnetic Radiation At Various Wavelengths' (1977) and 'Workshop Proceedings Of The 1978 U.S. Conference Of Research On The Shroud Of Turin' (3–4 June 1978). This material was of a preparatory nature but basically set forth what the scientists wished to accomplish with their tests.

Proposal to the Archbishop of Turin regarding Tests on the Holy Shroud, 24 April 1978.

1. *Dating the Shroud:*

A) A re-study in depth of the Carbon–14 Test (postponed for the present), since we do not have a consensus among the experts on the one-hundred-per cent efficacy of this Test in the specific case of the Shroud.

B) Since the Pollen Test has given very positive results with regard to the age and the history of the Shroud, we recommend that it be extended over a large area of the Shroud, and that it include part of the area of the reverse of the Shroud.

2. *On the nature and formation of the stains on the Shroud:*

A) Electronic microscopy with neutronic scansion and activation to determine the presence of blood or other substance on the Shroud. We suggest that for this test a sample be taken from the 'bloodstain' close to the feet on the dorsal imprint, outside the area of the imprint itself. The same process is suggested for samples taken from the area of the image or imprint.

B) Other suggested procedures: Radiographic examination – X-Ray fluorescent examination – micro-photography – infrared photographs – ultraviolet photographs – colour photographs – complete coverage with photographs in black and white, in whole or in sections.

C) Extensive examination of the reverse of the Shroud done with a flexible optical instrument so as not to have to unstitch the backing cloth from the Shroud, a process that would substantially damage the Shroud.

None of the above procedures would in any way damage the Shroud.

NB Approximate time needed and requested for these tests: 24 hours.

The material and information, including all original photographs, will be handed over to the Archbishop and will not be used without obtaining his approval.

This proposal has been formulated taking into account the suggestions made by the Scientific Commission of the USA Holy Shroud Guild.

The Scientific Commission of
the International Centre of Sindonology

List of the Official Members of the Testing Team (as given in *The Workshop Proceedings* of the United States Conference of Research on the Shroud of Turin at Colorado Springs, Colorado 3–4 June 1978)

Name	*Function*
Joseph Accetta, Air Force Weapons Laboratory	Coordinator: Infrared, X-Ray Fluorescence, Radiography
Donald Devan, Image Analysis, Information Science, Inc.	Coordinator: Photographic/Computer Enhancement and Analysis (PCEA)
The Revd. Robert Dinegar, Episcopal Priest, Physical Chemist, Los Alamos Laboratory	Chemical Consultant
Thomas D'Muhala, Attorney	Logistics Manager
Thomas Dolle, member of Christ Brotherhood, Santa Fe, New Mexico	Logistics Support Technician
John D. German, Major, USAF, Physicist/Electrical Engineer, Associate Professor, US Air Force Academy	Electronic Equipment Maintenance, Optical Spectrographic Examiner
Mrs John D. German	Logistics Support Technician
Thomas Haverty	Infrared
John Jackson, Capt. USAF, Physicist, Asst. Professor, US Air Force Academy	Project Coordinator

Mrs John Jackson	Logistics Support Technician
Donald Janney, Image Enhancement, Los Alamos Laboratory	PCEA
Eric Jumper, Capt. USAF, Asst. Professor of Aerodynamics, Air Force Academy	Project Coordinator
Mrs Eric Jumper	Logistics Support Technician
Ronald London	X-Ray Fluorescence, Radiography
Jean Lorre	PCEA
Donald Lynn, Image Enhancement, Jet Propulsion Laboratory	PCEA
Vernon Miller	Head Photographer
Roger Morris, Nondestructive Testing Engineer, Los Alamos Laboratory	Coordinator of X-Ray Fluorescence, Radiography, Infrared
William Mottern, Image Enhancement, Scandia Laboratory	Coordinator Radiography, Infrared
Father Otterbein	President, Holy Shroud Guild
Father Rinaldi	Vice President, Holy Shroud Guild
Ray Rogers, Archaeologist, Physical Chemist, Los Alamos Laboratory	Coordinator, Tape Sample Analysis, Chemical Consultant
Barrie Schwortz	Assistant Photographer
Kenneth Stevenson, IBM computer analyst, English Department, US Air Force Academy	Technical Recorder Secretary
Mrs Kenneth Stevenson	Logistics Support Technician

In January 1979 a proposal for carbon dating the Shroud according to the requirements stated at the October Congress was submitted to the Archbishop of Turin. The second laboratory for the test had been found – the Brookhaven National Laboratory at Upton, Long Island, New York. Brookhaven, founded in 1947 to explore the peaceful usages of atomic energy, has refined the conventional carbon test of Dr Libby using smaller samples than that technique normally requires. They were able to use 10mg of the 21mg carbon available from the larger of the Raes' samples. This would involve a counting time of two months. Harry Gove's laboratory could manage with 2mg of the available carbon content and an added attraction to the proposal was the fact that after its measurements, Brookhaven could make available the gas containing its 10mg of carbon to another laboratory using the cyclotron mechanism such as Lawrence Berkeley in California. (Carbon-dating scientists refer to the weight of carbon they require; this is about one-half the weight of the linen required to yield that weight of carbon).

The statements of Ray Rogers and others at the preparatory sessions for the October tests and at the Turin Congress that the Shroud images fluoresce seem to be based on a misunderstanding of information discussed at the New Mexico conference. Rogers' competent analysis, however, has raised important points to be considered with the assessment of the X-ray fluorescence test performed in October.

69. The Spanish sindonologist, Father Carreño Extreandia, SDB, has supplied me with helpful information on El Sagrado Rostro of Oviedo.

Chapter 8

70. Friends who work at New York's Metropolitan Museum have been very helpful with advice on discussing art forgery.
71. 'Objective' information on the Noah's Ark search is hard to come by. Probably the most balanced article I have seen appeared in the August 1975 issue of *The Christian Herald*. If one wishes to get the full flavour of the pursuit

he should try Tim F. La Haye and John D. Morris' *The Ark on Ararat* (Thomas Nelson, Inc. Nashville, Tennessee, 1976) from which I have quoted concerning the reasons for the exploration and the reaction to the carbon dating.
72. Joseph Hanlon, *The New Scientist*, 12 October 1978.
73. G. A. Wells, 'The Holy Shroud of Turin', *Question 9* (Dec. 1975), Rationalist Press, London.
74. Robert Dinegar, *The Proceedings Of The 1977 US Conference Of Research On The Shroud Of Turin*.

SCIENCE FACT FROM CORONET

ISAAC ASIMOV
- [ ] 19879 6 The Tragedy of the Moon — 60p
- [ ] 20015 4 Asimov on Astronomy — 80p
- [ ] 19999 7 Today and Tomorrow — 60p
- [ ] 19984 9 Please Explain — 85p

ADRIAN BERRY
- [ ] 19924 5 The Next Ten Thousand Years — £1.00

CARL SAGAN
- [ ] 19682 3 The Cosmic Connection — 85p

LYALL WATSON
- [ ] 18833 2 Supernature — £1.00
- [ ] 19989 X The Romeo Error — 80p
- [ ] 21974 2 Gifts Of Unknown Things — 85p

All these books are available at your local bookshop or newsagent, or can be ordered direct from the publisher. Just tick the titles you want and fill in the form below.

Prices and availability subject to change without notice.

CORONET BOOKS, P.O. Box 11, Falmouth, Cornwall.
Please send cheque or postal order, and allow the following for postage and packing:

U.K. – One book 22p plus 10p per copy for each additional book ordered, up to a maximum of 82p.

B.F.P.O. and EIRE – 22p for the first book plus 10p per copy for the next 6 Books, thereafter 4p per book.

OTHER OVERSEAS CUSTOMERS – 30p for the first book and 10p per copy for each additional book.

Name ....

Address ....

....